Level 8, Exten

C000203910

NEW MATHS FRAMEWORKING

Building process skills for KS3 and GCSE

Chris Pearce

Introduction

Welcome to *New Maths Frameworking*!

This workbook aims to help you reach a Level 8 in maths at Key Stage 3 and has hundreds of levelled questions to give you plenty of practice in the main areas of your course:

Number

Algebra

Shape, space and measure

Handling data

Smooth progression
Each topic allows you to practise your skills at Level 7 before moving on to try lots of Level 8 questions.

Levelled questions
Colour-coded National Curriculum levels for all the questions show you what level you are working at so you can easily track your progress and see how to get to the next level.

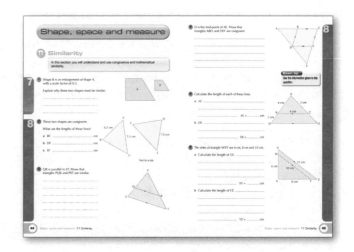

Review
The handy reviews at the end of each section let you assess your understanding of a mixture of topics.

Exam tip
Avoid common mistakes and remember the key points of a topic with the useful 'Exam tip' boxes.

Level progression maps
You can find level progression maps for the main subject areas on the Collins website. These show how you can move from a Level 7 to a Level 8 in each one. Use them to check what you know and what you need to practise more! www.collinseducation.com

Answers
Finally there are answers to all the questions at the back of the book. You can check your answers yourself or your teacher might tear them out and give to you later to mark your own work.

William Collins' dream of knowledge for all began with the publication of his first book in 1819. A self-educated mill worker, he not only enriched millions of lives, but also founded a flourishing publishing house. Today, staying true to this spirit, Collins books are packed with inspiration, innovation and practical expertise. They place you at the centre of a world of possibility and give you exactly what you need to explore it.

Collins. Freedom to teach.

Published by Collins
An imprint of HarperCollins*Publishers*
77–85 Fulham Palace Road
Hammersmith
London
W6 8JB

ISBN-13 978-0-00-743809-9

British Library Cataloguing in Publication Data
A Catalogue record for this publication is available from the British Library.
Commissioned by Katie Sergeant
Project managed by Emma Braithwaite
Edited by Joan Miller
Answers checked by Kay Macmullan and Joan Miller
Proofread by Joan Miller and Chris Pearce
Concept design by Jordan Publishing Design Limited
Design and typesetting by Hedgehog Publishing Ltd
Illustrations by Ann Paganuzzi
Cover design by Julie Martin
Production by Arjen Jansen
Printed and bound by Martins the Printers, Berwick upon Tweed

Browse the complete Collins catalogue at: www.collinseducation.com

Acknowledgements

The publishers wish to thank the following for permission to reproduce photographs. Every effort has been made to trace copyright holders and to obtain their permission for the use of copyright material. The publishers will gladly receive any information enabling them to rectify any error or omission at the first opportunity.

Cover image: The top end of a large crane ©shutterstock.com/Shi Yali

Contents

Number

1 Recurring decimals

In this section you will understand the equivalence between recurring decimals and fractions.

1 Work these out. **Do not use a calculator.**

 a $0.444 \times 10 =$ .... $0.4.44$ ....

 b $5.3535 \times 100 =$ .... 535.35 ....

 c $6.4222 \times 10 =$ .... 64.222 ....

 d $0.141\,414 \times 20 =$ .... $2.82\,828$ ....

2 Write the fractions in these calculations as decimals.

 a $\frac{2}{5} \times \frac{5}{8} = \frac{1}{4}$ .... × .... = ...

 b $2\frac{1}{4} \div 1\frac{7}{8} = 1\frac{1}{5}$ .... ÷ .... = ...

3 Work these out, giving your answers as fractions.

 a $\frac{5}{8} \times 10 =$ ....

 b $\frac{5}{8} \div 5 =$ ....

 c $\frac{5}{8} \div 2 =$ ....

 d $\frac{5}{8} \div \frac{1}{2} =$ ....

4 Write each of these mixed numbers as a decimal.

 a $2\frac{5}{8} =$ ....

 b $1\frac{8}{25} =$ ....

5 Write these fractions as recurring decimals.

 a $\frac{1}{6} =$ ....

 b $\frac{5}{6} =$ ....

 c $\frac{1}{9} =$ ....

 d $\frac{2}{9} =$ ....

 e $\frac{5}{9} =$ ....

 f $\frac{8}{9} =$ ....

6 $\frac{1}{3} = 0.\dot{3}$

Use this fact to write each of these fractions as a recurring decimal.

> **Exam tip**
>
> Remember that $0.\dot{3}$ means $0.3333\ldots$

 a $\frac{2}{3} =$ ....

 b $\frac{4}{3} =$ ....

 c $\frac{1}{30} =$ ....

 d $\frac{1}{6} =$ ....

7 Circle the fractions that are terminating decimals.

$\frac{3}{5}$ $\frac{5}{6}$ $\frac{2}{7}$ $\frac{1}{8}$ $\frac{4}{9}$ $\frac{3}{10}$ $\frac{11}{20}$ $\frac{7}{30}$ $\frac{49}{50}$

8 Write each of these fractions as a decimal.

 a $\frac{7}{8} =$ ....

 b $\frac{7}{9} =$ ....

 c $\frac{7}{11} =$ ....

 d $\frac{7}{12} =$ ....

9 $\frac{1}{7} = 0.\dot{1}4285\dot{7}$ and $\frac{2}{7} = 0.\dot{2}8571\dot{4}$.

Use these facts to write each of these fractions as a recurring decimal.

Exam tip

Dots are placed over the first and last digits of the repeating group

a $\frac{3}{7} =$ ....

b $\frac{6}{7} =$ ....

c $\frac{9}{7} =$ ....

d $\frac{50}{7} =$ ....

10 $\frac{3}{11} = 0.\dot{2}\dot{7}$

Write each of these fractions as a recurring decimal.

a $\frac{6}{11} =$ ....

b $\frac{1}{11} =$ ....

c $1\frac{3}{11} =$ ....

d $\frac{30}{11} =$ ....

11 $f = 0.\dot{7}\dot{5}$

a Write each of these as a recurring decimal.

   i $10f =$ ....

   ii $100f =$ ....

b Show that $99f$ is an integer.

....

c Use your answer to part **b** to write f as a fraction, in its simplest terms.

.... $f =$ ....

12 $f = 0.\dot{8}$

Work out the value of each expression in parts **a**, **b** and **c**.

a $10f =$ ....
b $5f =$ ....
c $9f =$ ....

d Use the answer to part **c** to write f as a fraction. .... $f =$ ....

13 $g = 0.3\dot{6}$

a Work out the value of $99g$. ....

   $99g =$ ....

b Write g as a fraction. .... $g =$ ....

14 Write $0.\dot{1}\dot{8}$ as a fraction, in its simplest terms.

....

.... $0.\dot{1}\dot{8} =$ ....

Exam tip

Show how you work out your answer.

15 Draw a line from each fraction to the corresponding decimal. One has been done for you.

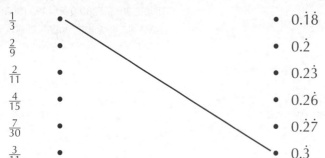

$\frac{1}{3}$ • • $0.1\dot{8}$

$\frac{2}{9}$ • • $0.\dot{2}$

$\frac{2}{11}$ • • $0.2\dot{3}$

$\frac{4}{15}$ • • $0.2\dot{6}$

$\frac{7}{30}$ • • $0.\dot{2}\dot{7}$

$\frac{3}{11}$ • • $0.\dot{3}$

16 Write $0.2\dot{6}$ as a fraction, in its simplest terms.

....

.... $0.2\dot{6} =$ ....

17 0.12112111211112111112...

Is this a recurring decimal? Give a reason for your answer.

....

18 Look at this pattern.

$\frac{1}{7} = 0.\dot{1}4285\dot{7}$

$\frac{2}{7} = 0.\dot{2}8571\dot{4}$

Use the pattern to write down $\frac{3}{7}$, $\frac{4}{7}$, $\frac{5}{7}$ and $\frac{6}{7}$ as decimals.

$\frac{3}{7} =$ .... $\frac{4}{7} =$ .... $\frac{5}{7} =$ .... $\frac{6}{7} =$ ....

19 Find, if possible, two recurring decimals that add up to a terminating decimal.

....

....

20 Find, if possible, two terminating decimals that add up to a recurring decimal.

....

....

21 $\frac{1}{3} = 0.\dot{3}$

Stan and Ollie are working out $\frac{1}{3} \times 3$.

Stan says that $\frac{1}{3} \times 3 = 1$ because it is $\frac{1}{3} + \frac{1}{3} + \frac{1}{3} = \frac{3}{3} = 1$.

Ollie says that $\frac{1}{3} \times 3 = 0.\dot{9}$ because $0.\dot{3} + 0.\dot{3} + 0.\dot{3} = 0.\dot{9}$.

Who is correct? Explain your answer. ....

....

② Proportional change

In this section you will:
- use fractions or percentages to solve problems involving repeated proportional changes
- calculate the original quantity, given the result of a proportional change.

1 a The price of a car was £12 650. The price is increased by 4%.
What is the new price?

.... £........................

b The price of a £460 washing machine is reduced by $\frac{1}{4}$ in a sale.
What is the sale price?

.... £........................

2 The value of an antique bought several years ago has multiplied by 1.6.
What is the percentage increase in value?

....%

3 'To decrease the price of an item by 15% in a single calculation, just multiply by ....'
Which of these is the correct missing multiplier? Circle it.

0.15   0.67   0.85   1.15   1.5

4 The mass of a baby is 4.00 kg. In a short time the mass increases by 20%. Then it increases by another 10%.

a What is the final mass? ....
....kg

b Show that the overall percentage increase is 32%.

....
....

5 A person invests £6000 and earns 4% interest each year for 3 years. What will the investment be worth after that time?

....

> **Exam tip**
> The multiplier method is the most efficient one for this type of question.

.... £........................

6 The area of weed in a lake increases by $\frac{1}{5}$ each week. At one point the area of weed is 6.00 m². What is the area of weed two weeks later?

....
....m²

8

7 The population of a town is 12 600 people. The population increases by 8% per year for 4 years. What is the population after that time? Give your answer to the nearest hundred.

....

....

8 The value of a car decreases by 15% a year. The value when it was new was £18 000.

a Work out the value of the car when it is:

i 1 year old .... £....................

ii 3 years old. .... £....................

b In how many years will the value be less than half the original value?

....

....

9 The value of a painting is £500.
The value increases by 20% every year for 3 years.

A calculation to find the value after 3 years is 500×1.2^3.

Write down a similar calculation to find the value of the painting in the following situations.

a The value increases by 30% a year for 2 years. ....

b The value decreases by 20% a year for 3 years. ....

c The value decreases by 30% a year for 2 years. ....

10 a The price of electricity increases by 10% and then falls by 5%.
What is the overall percentage change?

....

.... overall ....%

b Explain why an increase of 10% followed by a decrease of 5% is the same as a decrease of 5% followed by an increase of 10%.

....

....

11 A family is trying to reduce its carbon footprint by 5% a year.
If the family succeeds, what will be the overall reduction after 4 years?

....

.... overall ....%

12 Felling reduces the number of trees in a forest by 20% each year.
Nathan says that $5 \times 20\% = 100\%$ so after 5 years all the trees will be gone.

   a Explain why Nathan is incorrect. ....

   ....

   b What percentage of the trees will be left after 5 years? ....

   ....%

13 After 20% VAT is added onto a bill for servicing a car, the cost was £210.72.
What was the cost before adding VAT?

   .... £........................

14 In a sale, after a 60% reduction, the cost of a shirt was £18.
What was the original cost of the shirt?

   .... £........................

15 After spending two-fifths of her money, Jasmine had £54 left. How much did she start with?

   .... £........................

16 The population of a country is increasing by about 3% every 10 years. The current population
is 76.4 million. Use these figures to estimate the populations at the following times.
Give your answers to an appropriate degree of accuracy.

   a In 30 years' time ....

   ....

   b 10 years ago ....

   ....

17 a Find the single percentage change equivalent to the following.

   i An increase of 10% followed by a decrease of 10% ....

   ....%

   ii An increase of 20% followed by a decrease of 20% ....

   ....%

   iii An increase of 30% followed by a decrease of 30% ....

   ....%

   b Describe any pattern in your results from part **a**.

   ....

   ....

(3) Calculation problems

In this section you will solve problems involving calculating with powers, roots, and numbers expressed in standard form, checking for correct order of magnitude and using a calculator as appropriate.

(1) Estimate the value of each calculation by rounding each number to 1 significant figure.

a $37\,204 \times 0.315 =$ ....

b $6872 \div 0.494 =$ ....

c $0.0892 \times 0.030\,99 =$ ....

(2) **Use a calculator** to work out $\dfrac{28.5 + 43.7}{804.2 + 365.1}$. Give your answer to 2 significant figures.

....

(3) Write each of these as a single power of 7.

a $\dfrac{1}{7^2} =$ ....

b $\dfrac{7^3 \times 7^2}{7^6} =$ ....

> **Exam tip**
>
> You must learn the rules for multiplying and dividing powers.

c $(7^3)^3 =$ ....

d $7^{-2} \times 7^{-4} =$ ....

e $7^3 \div 7^{-2} =$ ....

(4) Write each of these as a fraction.

a $2^3 \times 3^{-2} =$ ....

b $8^{-2} \times 4^2 =$ ....

c $2^{-2} \div 5^2 =$ ....

(5) $72 = 2^c \times 3^d$ Find the values of c and d. ....

.... $c =$ .... $d =$ ....

(6) $54 \times 63 = 2 \times 7 \times 3^f$ Find the value of f. ....

.... $f =$ ....

(7) $\frac{1}{8} \times \frac{1}{16} = 2^k$.   Find the value of k. ....

.... $k =$ ....

(8) $\left(\frac{1}{1000}\right)^2 = 10^n$.   Find the value of n. ....

.... $n =$ ....

9 A billion is 10^9.

Write each of these numbers as a power of 10.

a one billionth = ... **b** (one billion)^2 = ...

10 Write each of these numbers in standard form.

a $420\,000$ = ... **b** $0.000\,000\,75$ = ...

c 746 million = ... **d** $\frac{27}{10\,000}$ = ...

e 300^2 = ... **f** 0.003×0.004 = ...

Use the information in this table for questions 11 to 13.

Planet	Mercury	Earth	Neptune
Average distance from the Sun (km)	5.79×10^7	1.50×10^8	4.50×10^9

11 Write the distance of Mercury from the Sun, in millions of kilometres.

.... million km

12 Write the distance of the Earth from the Sun, in metres, in standard form.

.... m

13 Neptune is N times further from the Sun than the Earth is. Find the value of N.

.... $N =$ ....

14 The mass of the Earth is 5.98×10^{24} kg.

The mass of the Moon is 7.35×10^{22} kg.

If the mass of the Moon is approximately $\frac{1}{N}$ of the mass of the Earth, find the value of the integer N.

.... $N =$ ....

15 Say whether these statements 'Could be true' or 'Must be false'.

a The height of a mountain is 3.5×10^6 km. ....

b The length of a piece of paper is 2.97×10^2 mm. ....

c The mass of a woman is 7.5×10^4 g. ....

d The distance from the Earth to the Moon is 3.845×10^{-5} km. ....

16 Draw lines between equivalent expressions.

The first one has been done for you.

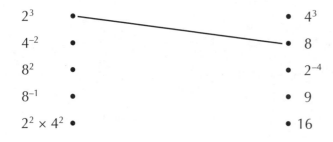

2^3 •

4^{-2} •

8^2 •

8^{-1} •

$2^2 \times 4^2$ •

$\frac{1}{3^{-2}}$ •

• 4^3

• 8

• 2^{-4}

• 9

• 16

• 2^{-3}

17 Write each of these numbers as a power of 6.

a $\sqrt{6}$ = ...

b $6(\sqrt[3]{6})^2$ = ...

c $\frac{1}{\sqrt[3]{6}}$ = ...

d $\frac{1}{36}$ = ...

18 Are these statements true or false? If they are false, give an example to show why.

a The square of a number is always positive. ....

....

b The square root of a number is less than or equal to the number. ....

....

c You can find the cube root of any number. ....

....

d N^{-2} is always less than N^2 if N is a positive number. ....

....

19 $A = 2.57 \times 10^5$ and $B = 6.43 \times 10^7$.

Use a calculator to find the value of each expression, giving your answer in standard form, correct to 3 significant figures.

a A^3 = ...

b $\sqrt[3]{B}$ = ...

c $\sqrt{A \times B}$ = ...

d $\frac{A^2}{B^2}$ = ...

1 The length of each side of a square is increased by 30%.
What is the percentage increase in the area of the square?

....%

2

Planet	Venus	Earth	Mars	Jupiter
Average distance from the Sun (D km)	1.082×10^8	1.496×10^8	2.279×10^8	7.783×10^8
Time to orbit the Sun (T days)	224.7	365.3	687	4332

Kepler's third law of planetary motion says that the value of $\dfrac{D^3}{T^2}$ is the same for any planet.

Check that this is the case for two planets of your choice, selected from the table.

....

....

....

3 **a** $\frac{7}{9} = 0.7777\ldots = 0.\dot{7}$ Use this fact to write each of these fractions as a recurring decimal.

i $\frac{7}{90} =$ ....

ii $\frac{7}{900} =$ ....

b $\frac{5}{9} = 0.5555\ldots = 0.\dot{5}$ Use this fact to write $\frac{1}{18}$ as a recurring decimal.

....

4 $\frac{5}{11} = 0.\dot{4}\dot{5}$

Use this fact to write the following fractions.

a $0.\dot{9}\dot{0} =$ ....   **b** $4.\dot{5}\dot{4} =$ ....   **c** $0.0\dot{4}\dot{5} =$ ....

5 **a** A number is multiplied by $\frac{10}{9}$.

i What is the fractional increase?   ....

ii What is the percentage increase?   ....

b The result is multiplied by another fraction and the answer is the original number.

i What is the second fraction?   ....

ii What is the percentage decrease?   ....

6 $48 \times 36 = 2^m \times 3^n$.

Find the value of m and n

....

.... $m =$ .... $n =$ ....

7 Without using a calculator, find the value of each expression.

a $\dfrac{5^2 \times 5^3}{(5^2)^3}$ .... $=$ ....

b $64^{\frac{1}{2}} \div 64^{\frac{1}{3}}$ .... $=$ ....

c $9^2 \times 9^{-2}$ .... $=$ ....

8 $\dfrac{1}{N}$ is a fraction, where N is a positive integer.

Explain how you can decide whether $\dfrac{1}{N}$ is a terminating decimal or a recurring decimal.

....

....

9 The price of petrol goes up by a quarter on three successive occasions. Show that the result is that the price has nearly doubled.

....

....

....

10 In 2010 the price of a car increased by 15%.

In 2011 the price decreased by 15%.

Ali said: 'The price is now back where it was at the start of 2010.'

Is Ali correct? What is the overall percentage change?

....

.... overall change $=$ ....

11 The distance to stars is measured in light years.
1 light year $= 9.46 \times 10^{12}$ km.

Exam tip

Your answer should not have more significant figures than the numbers you start with.

a The distance to the star Betelgeuse is 520 light years. Write this in kilometres, in standard form, to an appropriate number of significant figures.

....

.... km

b The fastest speed achieved by a space rocket is about 50 000 km/h. How long would it take such a rocket to reach Betelgeuse? Give your answer in years.

Exam tip
Show your working!

....

....

....

12 The wavelength of visible light is between 400 and 700 nanometres.

1 000 000 000 nanometres = 1 metre

Rewrite these two distances in metres, in standard form.

a 400 nanometres = ... m   **b** 700 nanometres = ... m

13 Sam found these two statements on the internet.

'A human hair is about one million carbon atoms wide.'

'The width of a human hair ranges from 20 to 200 micrometres.'

A micrometre is 10^{-6} metres.

Use these statements to estimate the width of a carbon atom, in metres.

....

.... width = ... m

14 A frog is jumping across a lawn. Each jump is 20% shorter than the previous one. The third jump was 10.5 cm long.

a How long was the fifth jump? ....

.... cm

b How long was the first jump? ....

.... cm

15

Year	1960	1970	1980	1990	2000	2010
World population (billions)	3.0	3.7	4.5	5.3	6.1	6.9

a Do the figures in this table show that the population of the world increases by the same proportion every ten years? Give evidence to support your answer.

....

....

....

b Estimate the world population in the year 2020. Show how you worked out your estimate.

....

....

Algebra

4 Quadratic expressions

In this section you will factorise quadratic expressions, including the difference of two squares.

7

1 Expand each of these expressions.

   a $x(x + 7) =$ .... $x^2 + 7x$ ....

   b $(x - 5)x =$ .... $x^2 - 5x$ ....

2 Expand and simplify each of these expressions.

   a $(x + 4)(x - 6) =$ $x^2 - 6x + 4x - 24 \to x^2 - 2x - 24$

   b $(x + 3)(x - 5) =$ $x^2 - 5x + 3x - 15 \to x^2 - 12x - 15$

   c $(x + 9)(x - 10) =$ $x^2 - 10x + 9x - 90 \to x^2 - x - 90$

   d $(x - 2)(x - 7) =$ $x^2 - 2x - 7x + 14 \to x^2 - 9x + 14$

                      $-2 + -7 = -9$

3 Expand and simplify each expression.

   a $(x + 4)^2 =$ .... $x^2 + 16$ ....

   b $(x - 5)^2 =$ .... $x^2 + 25$ ....

8

4 Factorise each expression.

   a $x^2 + 6x + 8 =$ ....

   b $x^2 - 6x + 8 =$ ....

   c $x^2 + 11x =$ ....

   d $x^2 + 2x - 15 =$ ....

   e $x^2 + 4x - 21 =$ ....

   f $x^2 - x - 30 =$ ....

   g $x^2 + 19x - 20 =$ ....

   h $x^2 - 10x + 16 =$ ....

5 The area of a rectangle is $x^2 + 9x + 18$.

The length of one side is $x + 3$.

How long is the other side?

$x + 3$

....

6 Draw lines between matching expressions. The first one has been done for you.

$x^2 + 8x + 12$ •

$x^2 - 11x - 12$ •

$x^2 + 4x - 12$ •

$x^2 + x - 12$ •

$x^2 - 13x + 12$ •

• $(x + 4)(x - 3)$

• $(x + 6)(x + 2)$

• $(x - 1)(x - 12)$

• $(x - 2)(x + 6)$

• $(x + 3)(x - 4)$

• $(x - 12)(x + 1)$

7 Factorise each expression.

a $x^2 + 4 =$ $(x-2)^2$

b $x^2 + 16 =$ $(x-4)^2$

c $x^2 + 100 =$ $(x-10)^2$

d $x^2 + 625 =$ $(x-25)^2$

8 Explain why $9999^2 - 1$ is the same as $10\,000 \times 9998$.

$9999^2 - 1 = 99,980,000$

$10\,000 \times 9998 = 99,980,000$

9 **a** A and B are two consecutive integers.

$A^2 - B^2 = 35$. $A^2B^2 = \uparrow 35$ $A = 6$ $B = 1$

What is $A + B$? $36 - 1 = 35$

A is 6 and B is 1

Exam tip

What does 'consecutive' mean?

b Now generalise your answer to part **a**.

10 $(x - 5)(x + p) = x^2 - qx - 10$.

Find the values of p and q.

$p =$ .... $q =$ ....

11 $(x - 4)(x - r) = x^2 - 7x + s$.

Find the values of r and s.

....

.... $r =$ .... $s =$ ....

12 **a** Factorise $x^2 - y^2$. ....

b Use factors to show that $26^2 - 24^2 = 100$.

....

....

c P and Q are integers that differ by 2 and $P^2 - Q^2 = 200$.

Find the values of P and Q.

....

.... $P =$ .... $Q =$ ....

13 Explain why it is impossible to find two integers a and b so that $x^2 + 3x - 6 = (x + a)(x - b)$.

....

....

14 $x^2 + px - 18 = (x + a)(x + b)$ where a and b are integers.

How many different possible values for p are there?

....

....

15 The area of the large square is a^2.

The area of the small square is b^2.

Rearrange the shaded parts of the diagram to show that
$a^2 - b^2 = (a + b)(a - b)$.

Show your solution below.

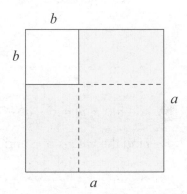

⑤ Algebraic manipulation

In this section you will manipulate algebraic formulae, equations and expressions, finding common factors and multiplying two linear expressions.

① Solve simultaneously these two equations.

$2x + 3y = 55$

$y = 3x$

....

....

.... $x =$ .... $y =$ ....

② Solve simultaneously these two equations.

$4x + 5y = 52$

$4x - 5y = 12$

....

....

.... $x =$ .... $y =$ ....

③ Factorise each expression as much as possible.

a $3x^2 + 9x =$ ....

b $10a^2 - 4a^3 =$ ....

c $16a^2b - 12ab^2 =$ ....

④ Simplify each expression.

a $3(x - 5) + 5(x + 4) =$ ....

b $12 - (7 - x) =$ ....

c $5(m + 4) - 2(m - 10) =$ ....

d $x(x - 2) + x(x - 3) =$ ....

e $4k - 5(k - 2) =$ ....

5 Multiply these brackets and simplify each expression as much as possible.

a $(2x + 3)(2x - 1) =$ ....

b $(5a - 2)(3a + 4) =$ ....

c $(3x + 7)(3x - 7) =$ ....

d $(2 - a)(5 - a) =$ ....

e $(2m + 3)^2 =$ ....

6 Simplify each expression as much as possible.

a $(x + 4)^2 - (x + 2)^2 =$ ....

b $(2a - 3)^2 - (1 - 2a)^2 =$ ....

7 Show that $(s + t)^2 - (s - t)^2 = 4st$.

....

....

8 Here is an incorrect attempt to solve an equation.

$$2(x - 2) - 3(6 - x) = 2(x + 2)$$

$$\Rightarrow \quad 2x - 4 - 18 - 3x = 2x + 2$$

$$\Rightarrow \quad -x - 22 = 2x + 2$$

$$\Rightarrow \quad -3x = 24$$

$$\Rightarrow \quad x = -8$$

a By substituting $x = -8$ into each side of the original equation, show that this solution is incorrect.

$2(x - 2) - 3(6 - x) =$ ....

$2(x + 2) =$ ....

b Correct the mistakes and write out the steps of a correct solution.

....

....

....

....

9 Solve this equation. $\dfrac{2x+3}{4} = \dfrac{5x-3}{3}$

....

....

.... $x = ...$

10 Solve this equation. $\dfrac{x}{2} + \dfrac{3x}{4} = 15$

....

....

.... $x = ...$

11 Write each expression as a single fraction.

a $\dfrac{2x}{5} + \dfrac{1}{10} =$ ....

b $\dfrac{2x-1}{2} - \dfrac{x+2}{4} =$ ....

12 $8x^2 - ex - 15 = (4x + c)(dx - 3)$

Find the values of c, d and e.

....

....

.... $c = ...$ $d = ...$ $e = ...$

13 Simplify each expression.

a $\dfrac{x^2 + 5x + 6}{x + 3} =$ ....

....

b $\dfrac{x^2 - 25}{x - 5} =$ ....

....

c $\dfrac{4(x+5) + 2(x-4)}{x+2} =$ ....

....

14 a What goes in the second set of brackets to complete these factorisations?

    i $x^2 + x - 6 = (x - 2)(\ldots\ldots)$ ....

    ii $x^2 + x - 6 = (\frac{1}{2}x - 1)(\ldots\ldots)$ ....

    iii $x^2 + x - 6 = (2x - 4)(\ldots\ldots)$ ....

b How could the results in part **a** be generalised to give further factorisations of the expression $x^2 + x - 6$?

....

....

....

15 Factorise, as much as possible, the expression $3a^3 - 21a^2 + 30a$.

....

....

....

16 a Show that $(2a + 1)^2 - (a + 2)^2 = 3(a + 1)(a - 1)$.

....

....

....

b Find a similar expression for $(3a + 1)^2 - (a + 3)^2$.

....

....

....

17 $\dfrac{x^2 - 7x + 12}{x + a} = x + b$, where a and b are integers.

Find all possible values of a and b.

....

....

....

⑥ Deriving formulae

In this section you will:
- derive and use more complex formulae
- change the subject of a formula.

① A formula you may use in physics is $E = I^2R$.

   a Find the value of E if $I = 0.15$ and $R = 70$.

.... $E =$ ....

   b Make R the subject of the formula.

.... $R =$ ....

② This is a right-angled triangle.

   a Write down a formula for the perimeter, P, simplifying it as much as possible.

.... $P =$ ....

   b Write down a formula for the area, A, of the triangle.

.... $A =$ ....

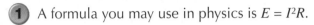

③ Engineers often use the formula $A = \dfrac{\pi d^2}{4}$ for the area, A, of a circle in terms of the diameter, d.

   a Show that this formula is equivalent to the usual formula for A in terms of the radius, r.

....

Exam tip

You must memorise the formulae for the circumference and area of a circle. You will not be given them.

   b Make d the subject of the formula.

....

.... $d =$ ....

④ A formula you may use in mechanics is $v^2 = u^2 + 2as$.

   a Make s the subject of this formula.

....

.... $s =$ ....

   b Make u the subject of this formula.

....

.... $u =$ ....

8

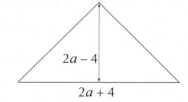

5 These rectangles have the same perimeter.
Work out the value of *a*.

$a =$ ....

....

....

a + 4

a $\boxed{}$

2a + 1 $\boxed{}$ 2a

a = ...

6 The length of the base of a triangle is $2a + 4$
and the height is $2a - 4$.

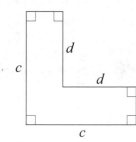

a Show that the area, *A*, of the triangle is given by
the formula $A = 2(a^2 - 4)$.

....

....

b Make *a* the subject of the formula.

....

.... *a* = ...

7 By considering the area of this shape, show that:
$c^2 - d^2 = (c + d)(c - d)$.

....

....

....

....

....

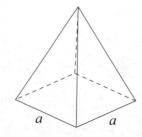

c, d, d, c

8 $V = \frac{1}{3}a^2h$

This is the formula for the volume, *V*, of a pyramid
with a square base of side *a* and height *h*.

a Make *h* the subject of this formula.

....

.... *h* = ...

b Make *a* the subject of this formula.

....

.... *a* = ...

9 This is a quarter of a circle.
Show that a formula for the perimeter P is:

$P = \frac{1}{2}r(\pi + 4)$

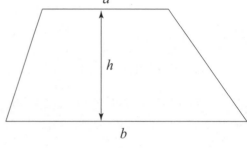

....

....

....

10 The area, A, of this trapezium is given by
the formula:

$A = \frac{1}{2}(a + b)h$

a Make h the subject of this formula.

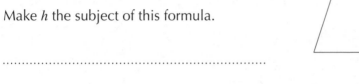

....

....

.... $h = $ ....

b Make b the subject of this formula.

....

....

.... $b = $ ....

c For a particular trapezium $b = 2a$ and $h = \frac{3}{4}a$.

Write a formula for the area of this trapezium in terms of a.

....

.... $a = $ ....

11 Fran is f years old and George is g years old. Fran is older than George.
The sum of their ages is three times the difference between their ages.

a Write a formula to express this fact. ....

....

b Show that Fran is twice as old as George. ....

....

....

8

12 Two circles of equal radius just fit inside a circle of radius r.

Show that a formula for the area, A, of the shaded part of the diagram is:

$A = \frac{1}{2}\pi r^2$

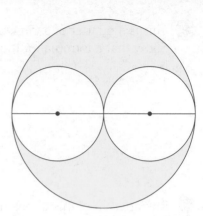

....

....

....

13 $T = 2\pi\sqrt{\dfrac{l}{k}}$

This is the formula for the time, T, for a pendulum of length l to make one oscillation.

Make l the subject of this formula.

....

.... $l =$ ....

14 In question 9 you showed that a formula for the perimeter of a quarter of a circle is

$P = \frac{1}{2}r(\pi + r)$.

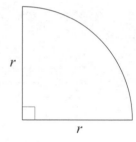

Simon says that a semicircle is twice the size so the perimeter will be doubled to give

$P = r(\pi + r)$.

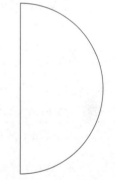

a Explain why Simon is not correct.

....

....

....

b Find a correct formula for the perimeter of a semicircle.

....

....

.... $P =$ ....

Evaluating formulae

In this section you will evaluate algebraic formulae, substituting fractions, decimals and negative numbers.

1 $S = 2(ab + bc + ca)$

This is the formula for the surface area, S, of a cuboid with sides a, b and c units.

Calculate the value of S if $a = 4$, $b = 5$ and $c = 7$.

.... $S =$ ....

2 $V = \frac{1}{3}a^2h$

This is the formula for the volume, V, of a pyramid with a square base of side a and height h.

Calculate the value of V if $a = 5$ and $h = 8$.

.... $V =$ ....

3 A formula you may use in physics is $s = ut + \frac{1}{2}at^2$.

Find the value of s if $u = 35$, $a = -1.6$ and $t = 7.5$.

.... $s =$ ....

4 The number $3\frac{1}{7}$ is sometimes used as a value for π. Use this value to work out the circumference of a circle with a radius of $1\frac{3}{4}$ cm.

.... circumference = ... cm

5 This is a square-based pyramid with the top removed. It is called a frustum.

The height of the frustum is h. The volume, V,

of the frustum is given by the formula $V = \frac{h}{3}(a^2 + ab + b^2)$.

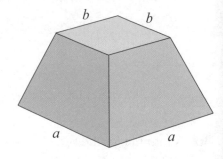

a Show that, if $b = 0$, the formula for the volume of a frustum is the same as the formula for the volume of a pyramid in question **2**.

....

b Does this prove that the formula for the volume of a frustum is correct? Give a reason for your answer.

....

c Find the volume of a frustum if $a = 5.7$ cm, $b = 3.8$ cm and $h = 4.3$ cm.

....

.... $V =$ .... cm³

8

6 A formula for the length of <u>side c in this triangle</u>, in terms of a and b, is $c = \sqrt{a^2 + b^2 - \sqrt{3}ab}$.

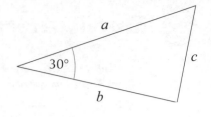

Find the value of c if $a = 3.5$ and $b = 4.5$.

....

.... $c = ...$

7 A formula for the volume, V, of a sphere of radius r is $V = \frac{4}{3}\pi r^3$.

A spherical balloon is being blown up. The radius increases from 9 cm to 15 cm.
Work out the increase in volume.

....

.... cm^3

8 The geometric mean, g, of three numbers, a, b and c, is given by the formula $g = \sqrt[3]{abc}$.

Calculate the geometric mean of 14.5, 16.5 and 18.5.

....

.... $g = ...$

9 A formula used with lenses is $\frac{1}{f} = \frac{1}{g} + \frac{1}{h}$.

Use this formula to find the value of f when $g = 23$ and $h = 37$.

....

....

.... $f = ...$

10 A formula for the surface area, S, of a cylinder of radius r and height h is $S = 2\pi r(r + h)$.

Find the value of S if $r = 2.7$ and $h = 8.3$.

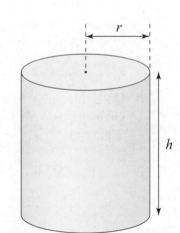

....

....

....

.... $S = ...$

11 A cone has a base radius of r and a height of h. A formula for the total surface area, C, of the cone is $C = \pi r(r + \sqrt{r^2 + h^2})$.

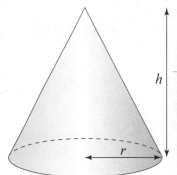

Work out the value of C if $r = 4.5$ and $h = 12.5$.

....

....

....

.... C = ...

12 This 3-D shape is called a torus.

A formula for its volume is $\frac{1}{4}\pi^2(a + b)(a - b)^2$.

a Calculate the volume, if $a = 5.7$ cm and $b = 3.2$ cm.

....

....

....

.... volume = ... cm^3

b If $a = 2b$, write the volume in terms of b, as simply as possible.

....

....

....

....

.... volume = ... cm^3

13 The area of a regular hexagon of side a is $\frac{3\sqrt{3}}{2}a^2$.

This shape is made from regular hexagons of side $3\frac{1}{3}$ cm.

Calculate its area.

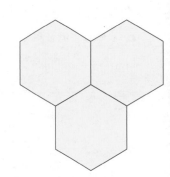

....

....

....

.... area = ... cm^2

⑧ Inequalities

In this section you will solve inequalities in two variables and find the solution set.

7

① **a** Solve the inequality $3x - 7 \geqslant -1$.

....

b Show the solution set on this number line.

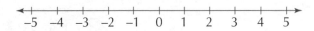

② Solve the inequality $x^2 < 9$.

....

....

....

8

③ Show, by shading, the region where $2 \leqslant x \leqslant 5$ and $1 \leqslant y \leqslant 3$.

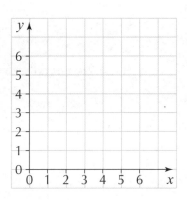

④ Which point on the graph satisfies both inequalities?

a $x \geqslant 2$ and $y \geqslant 2$ ....

b $x < 1$ and $y > -1$ ....

c $x \leqslant 0$ and $y \leqslant 1$ ....

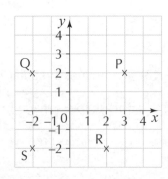

5 Write down three inequalities that describe the shaded region.

The boundary lines should be included.

Exam tip

Start with the equations of
the lines.

....

....

....

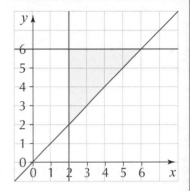

6 The equation of the curved line is $y = 4 - x^2$.

Write down two inequalities to describe the shaded region.

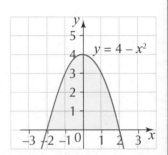

....

....

7 The two lines divide the graph into four regions.
One point is marked in each region

Write A, B, C or D next to the appropriate pair of
inequalities.

a $x + 2y \leqslant 6$ and $2x + y \leqslant 8$ ....

b $x + 2y \leqslant 6$ and $2x + y \geqslant 8$ ....

c $x + 2y \geqslant 6$ and $2x + y \leqslant 8$ ....

d $x + 2y \geqslant 6$ and $2x + y \geqslant 8$ ....

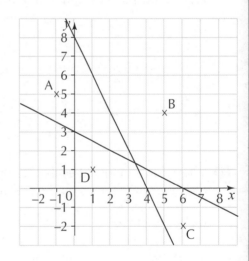

8 These three inequalities describe a region.

$$x + y \geqslant 0 \qquad y \leqslant x \qquad x \leqslant 5$$

State whether each point given below is inside, outside or on the boundary of the region.

a (4, 4) ....

b (7, 3) ....

c (3, −2) ....

d (−1, 1) ....

9 Here are three inequalities.

$x \geqslant 2$ $\qquad$ $y \geqslant 3$ $\qquad$ $x + y \leqslant 4$

a Explain why there is no solution set for these inequalities.

....

....

....

....

b What happens if the third inequality is changed to $x + y \leqslant 5$?

....

....

....

....

10 M and N are integers. $M < 8$, $N < 9$ and $M + N > 11$.

How many pairs of values of M and N are there in the solution set?

....

....

....

.... pairs

11 Write down inequalities that describe as fully as possible the following regions on the graph.

a Rectangle A $\quad$ ....

b Triangle B $\quad$ ....

c Trapezium C $\quad$ ....

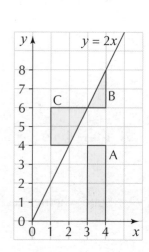

Graphs

In this section you will sketch, identify and interpret graphs of linear, quadratic, cubic and reciprocal functions, and graphs that model real situations.

1 **a** Complete this table of values for $y = x^2 - 5$.

x	–3	–2	–1	0	1	2	3
y	4			–5			

b Plot the graph of $y = x^2 - 5$ for $-3 \leqslant x \leqslant 3$.

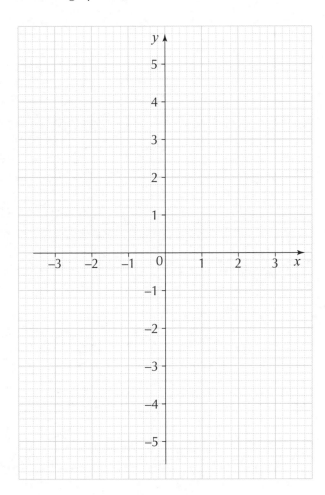

7

② Draw the graph of $y = x^3$ for $-2 \leq x \leq 2$.

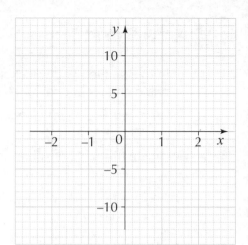

8

③ **a** Complete this table of values for $y = x^2 - 3x$.

x	−1	0	1	2	3	4
y	4			−2		

b Draw the graph of $y = x^2 - 3x$.

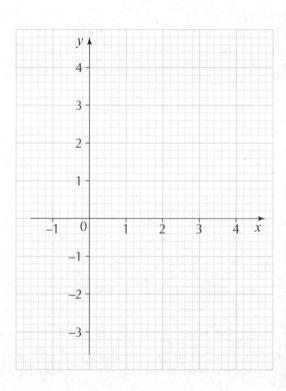

c The graph has a line of symmetry.

Write down its equation.   ....

4 **a** Complete this table of values for $y = \dfrac{10}{x}$.

x	2	3	4	5
y				

b Draw the graph of $y = \dfrac{10}{x}$ for $2 \leqslant x \leqslant 5$.

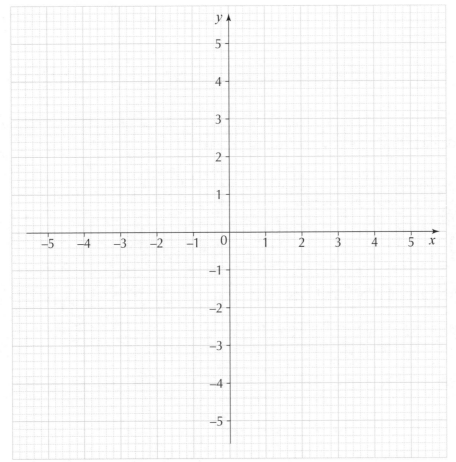

c Sketch, on the same axes, the graph of $y = \dfrac{10}{x}$ for $-5 \leqslant x \leqslant -2$.

5 Write down the letter of the correct graph for each equation.

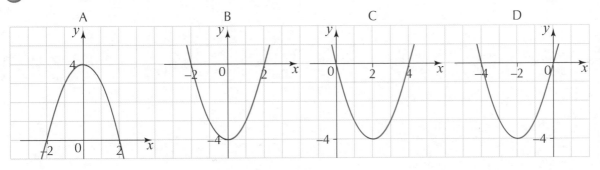

a $y = x^2 - 4x$ .... **b** $y = 4 - x^2$ .... **c** $y = 4x + x^2$ ....

6 Sketch the graph of $y = (x - 2)(x - 4)$ for $0 \leqslant x \leqslant 6$.

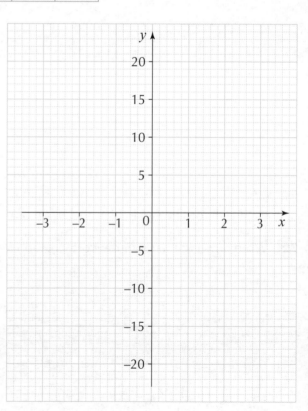

7 a Complete this table of values for $y = x^3 - 4x$.

x	−3	−2	−1	0	1	2	3
y	−15						15

b Draw the graph of $y = x^3 - 4x$.

c Describe the symmetry of the graph.

....

....

....

8 A rectangle has an area of 100 cm². The length is l cm.

a Explain why the width, w, can be calculated as $w = \dfrac{100}{l}$.

....

....

....

b Sketch a graph to show how w varies with l.

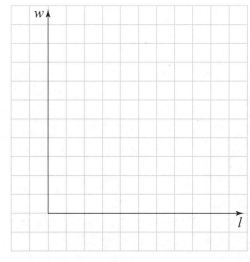

9 Sketch a graph to show how the area, A, of a circle varies with the radius, r.

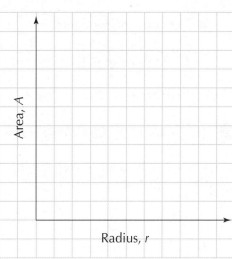

10 Transforming graphs

In this section you will understand the effect on a graph of addition of (or multiplication by) a constant.

7

1 Here are graphs of $y = x^2$ and $y = x^3$.

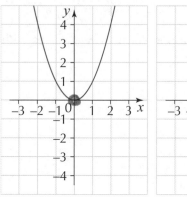 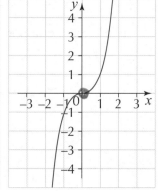

a Which points are common to both graphs?

0, 0

....

....

b Describe the symmetry of each graph.

i $y = x^2$ ....

ii $y = x^3$ ....

8

2 This is a sketch of the line $y = x$.

On the same axes, sketch the lines with these equations.

a $y = 0.5x$

b $y = x + 3$

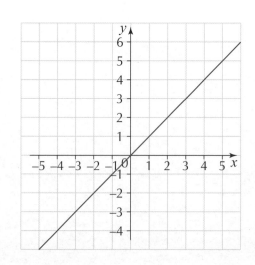

3 This is a graph of $y = x^2 - 2x$.

On the same axes, sketch the graph of $y = x^2 - 2x + 2$.

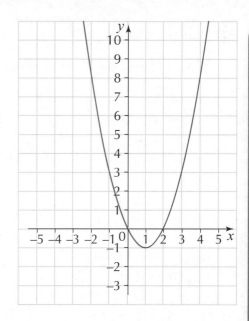

4 This is a graph of $y = 0.2x^3$.

On the same axes, sketch the graph of $y = 0.1x^3$.

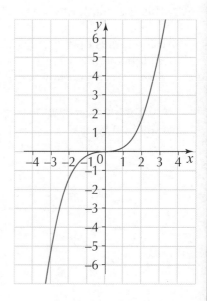

5 This is a graph of $y = \sqrt{x}$.

On the same axes, draw the graph of:

a $y = 2\sqrt{x}$

b $y = \sqrt{x} - 3$.

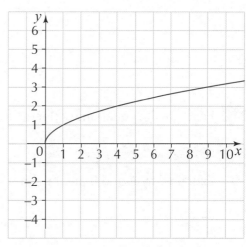

6 This is a graph of $y = \frac{8}{x}$.

On the same axes, sketch a graph of:

a $y = \frac{8}{x} - 2$ **b** $y = \frac{16}{x}$.

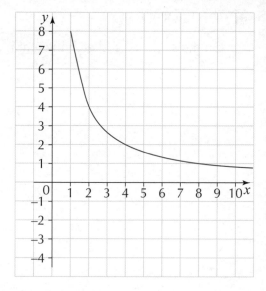

7 This is a graph of $y = x^2$.

If the radius of a circle is x cm and the area is y cm^2, then you can write $y = \pi x^2$.

Sketch the curve with equation $y = \pi x^2$.

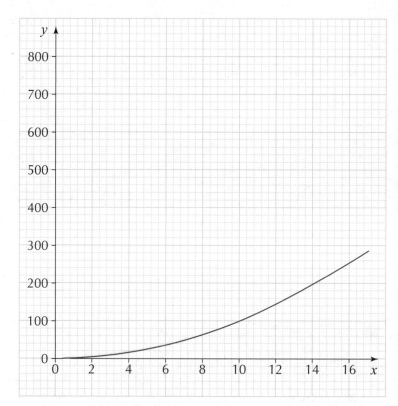

8 Here are the equations of three curves.

A: $y = x^3$ B: $y = x^3 + 3$ C: $y = 3x^3$

Explain why A and B are the same shape but A and C are not.

....

....

....

1 Factorise each expression.

   a $x^2 - 81 =$ ....

   b $x^2 + 24x - 81 =$ ....

   c $x^2 - 80x - 81 =$ ....

2 Simplify as much as possible $(2x + 1)(2x + 3) - 4x(x + 1)$.

....

....

....

3   **a** Factorise $x^2 + x - 12$.

....

....

   b Where does the graph of $y = x^2 + x - 12$ cross the y-axis?   ....

   c Where does the graph of $y = x^2 + x - 12$ cross the x-axis?   ....

   d Where does the graph of $y = 2(x^2 + x - 12)$ cross the y-axis?   ....

   e Where does the graph of $y = 2(x^2 + x - 12)$ cross the x-axis?   ....

4 Solve each equation.

   a $\dfrac{x}{2} + \dfrac{x}{3} = 30$

....

.... $x =$ ....

   b $\dfrac{2x + 1}{5} = \dfrac{2x - 5}{3}$

....

.... $x =$ ....

5 **a** Show that $x^2 - 4x = (x - 2)^2 - 4$.

....

....

....

b This is a graph of $y = (x - 2)^2$.

Use it to help you sketch a graph of $y = x^2 - 4x$.

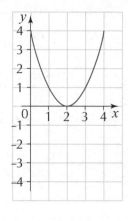

6 Simplify $\dfrac{x^2 + 3x - 10}{x^2 - 6x + 8}$.

....

....

....

7 Engineers sometimes use a formula connecting the area, A, and circumference, C, of a circle, which is $A = \dfrac{C^2}{4\pi}$.

a Make C the subject of this formula.

....

....

.... $C =$ ....

b A formula for the circumference of a circle is $C = 2\pi r$, where r is the radius.
Use this and the formula above to deduce the more usual formula for the area of a circle.

....

....

....

....

8 The equation of one line on this graph is $y = x^3 - 4x$.

   a What is the equation of the other line?

   ....

   b On the same axes, sketch the graph of $y = \frac{1}{2}(x^3 - 4x)$.

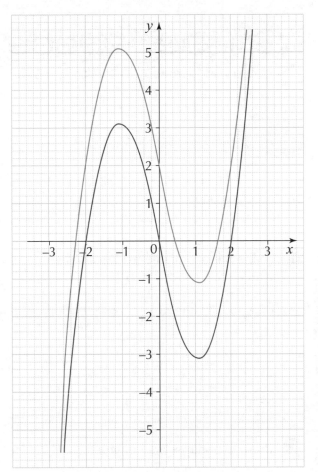

9

     A   B   C   D

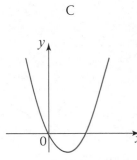 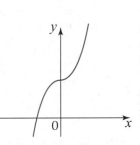

Match the equations to the graphs.

   a $y = x^2 - 2x$ ....
      b $y = x^2 + 2x$ ....

   c $y = x^3 + 2$ ....
      d $y = x^3 + 2x^2$ ....

Shape, space and measure

11 Similarity

In this section you will understand and use congruence and mathematical similarity.

7

1 Shape B is an enlargement of shape A, with a scale factor of 0.5.

Explain why these two shapes must be similar.

....

....

....

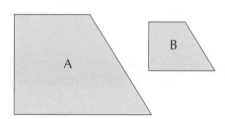

8

2 These two shapes are congruent.

What are the lengths of these lines?

a BC .... cm

b DF .... cm

c EF .... cm

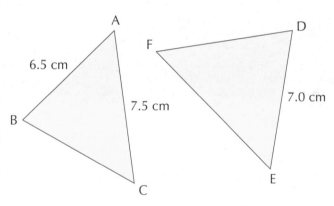

Not to scale

3 QR is parallel to ST. Prove that triangles PQR and PST are similar.

....

....

....

....

....

....

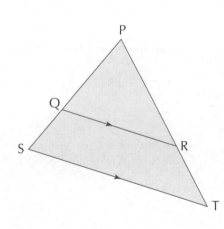

4 D is the mid-point of AE. Prove that triangles ABD and DEF are congruent.

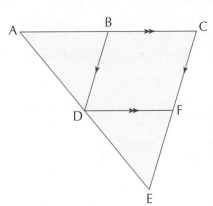

....

....

....

....

....

Exam tip

Use the information given in the question.

5 Calculate the length of each of these lines.

a AE ....

....

.... AE = ... cm

b DE ....

....

.... DE = ... cm

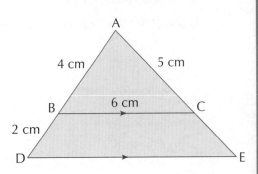

6 The sides of triangle WXY are 6 cm, 8 cm and 10 cm.

a Calculate the length of XV. ....

....

....

....

.... XV = ... cm

b Calculate the length of YZ. ....

....

....

....

.... YZ = ... cm

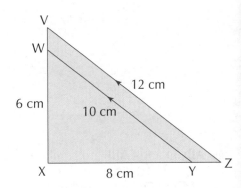

8

7 **a** Here are two statements.

    1 All equilateral triangles are similar.

    2 All isosceles triangles are similar.

    Explain why the first statement is **true** but the second statement is **false**.

....

....

....

....

b Here is a third statement.

    3 All right-angled isosceles triangles are similar.

    Is this statement true or false? Give a justification of your answer.

....

....

....

....

8 These two rectangles are similar.

Calculate the area of the small rectangle.

....

....

....

.... area = ... cm²

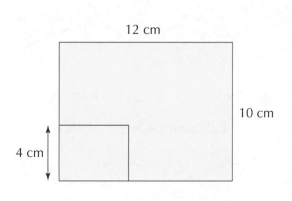

12 cm

10 cm

4 cm

9 ABCD and EABF are similar rectangles.

AD and DE are 5 cm long.

Prove that the length of AB is $\sqrt{50}$ cm.

....

....

....

....

A   B

5 cm

D   C

5 cm

E   F

⑫ Trigonometry

In this section you will:
- understand and use trigonometrical relationships in right-angled triangles
- use these to solve problems, including those involving bearings.

① Calculate the lengths of the unlabelled sides in each of these triangles.

a ....
....
.... cm

b ....
....
.... cm

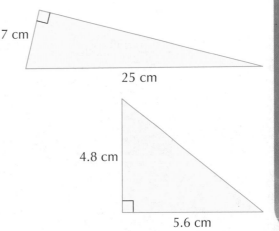

7 cm

25 cm

4.8 cm

5.6 cm

② Calculate the size of the angle at A in each triangle.

a ....
....
....°

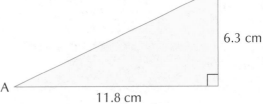

6.3 cm

A

11.8 cm

b ....
....
....°

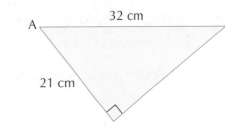

A

32 cm

21 cm

c ....
....
....°

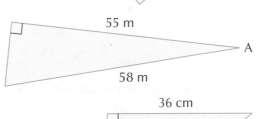

55 m

A

58 m

d ....
....
....°

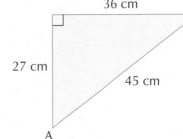

36 cm

27 cm

45 cm

A

8

3 Calculate the values of *a*, *b*, *c* and *d*.

a ....

.... *a* = ...

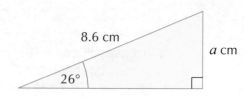

b ....

.... *b* = ...

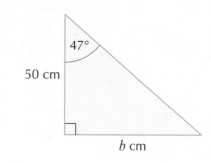

c ....

.... *c* = ...

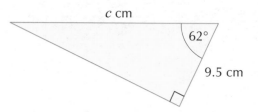

d ....

.... *d* = ...

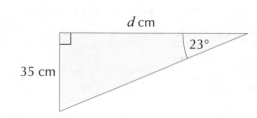

4 A metre ruler is leaning against a wall.

The lower end of the ruler is 15 cm from the wall.

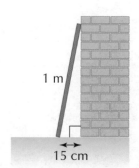

a Calculate the angle between the ruler and the wall.

....

....

....°

b How high above the floor is the top of the ruler?

....

....

.... cm

5 Is it possible to have a triangle with these dimensions?

Give a reason for your answer.

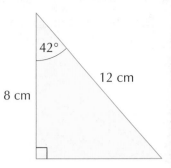

....

....

....

6 Here is a true statement.

> • If you know two sides of a right-angled triangle you can calculate all the angles of the triangle.

Explain why this statement is true.

....

....

7 **a** Find the length of the third side of this triangle.

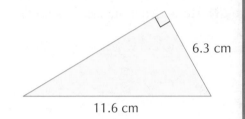

....

....

.... cm

b Find the size of the smallest angle of the triangle.

....

....

....°

8 **a** Calculate the length of AC.

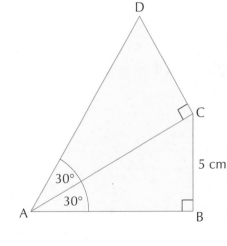

....

....

.... AC = ... cm

b Calculate the length of CD.

....

....

.... CD = ... cm

8

9 A boat travels 15 km on a bearing of 305°.
How far north does the boat travel?

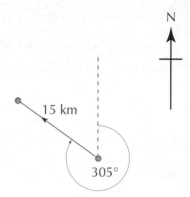

....

....

....

.... distance north = ... km

10 A church is 5.5 km east and 2.4 km south of a tower.

Calculate the bearing of the church from the tower.

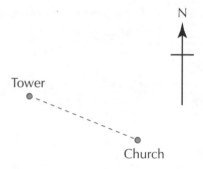

....

....

....

.... bearing = ...°

11 These two triangles are similar.

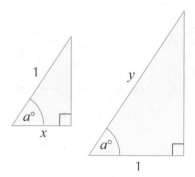

   a Explain why $x = \cos a°$.

   ....

   ....

   ....

   b Explain why $y = \dfrac{1}{\cos a°}$.

   ....

   ....

   ....

12 ABCDE is a regular polygon of side 50 cm.

Calculate the length of the diagonal AC.

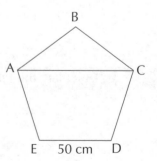

....

....

....

.... AC = ...cm

(13) Dimensions

> In this section you will understand the difference between formulae for perimeter, area and volume in simple contexts by considering dimensions.

(1) This is a triangular prism with a right-angled cross-section.

A formula for the surface area is $A = l(a + b + c) + ab$.

A formula for the volume is $V = \frac{1}{2}abl$.

Calculate the following when $a = 3$, $b = 4$, $c = 5$ and $l = 10$.

The lengths are in centimetres. Put units in your answers.

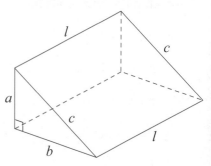

a The surface area ....

....

....

b The volume ....

....

....

(2) Three lengths on an object are p cm, q cm and r cm.

The following formulae are for a length, an area or a volume.

In each case, state whether it is a length, an area or a volume.

Then work out the value if $p = 7$ and $q = 5$ and $r = 4$. Put units in your answers.

a πpq is ....

Its value = ...

b $3p + 4q$ is ....

Its value = ...

c $\frac{1}{2}(p + q)(p - q)$ is ....

Its value = ...

d $p^2(p + q)$ is ....

Its value = ...

e $pq + qr + rp$ is ....

Its value = ...

8

3 A solid piece of wood is carved in the shape of a hemisphere (half a sphere) with a radius of r cm.

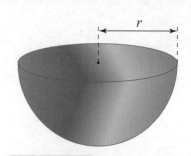

Formulae for the length of the rim, the volume and the surface area, not necessarily in that order, are $\frac{2}{3}\pi r^3$, $3\pi r^2$ and $2\pi r$.

Calculate the following when $r = 6$, leaving π in your answer each time. Give units for each answer.

a the length of the rim ....

....

> **Exam tip**
>
> This is called 'leaving your answer in terms of π'.

b the volume ....

c the surface area ....

4 The perimeter and area of this shape are given by the formulae $\frac{1}{2}a(4 + \pi)$ and $\frac{1}{4}a^2(4 - \pi)$.

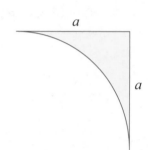

How can you tell which is the perimeter formula and which is the area formula?

....

....

5 Here are five formulae.

$$2(a^2 + b^2 + c^2) \qquad ab + bc \qquad (a + b + c)^2 \qquad a^2b + b^2c \qquad (a + b)(a + c)$$

The letters a, b and c all represent lengths. Which formula is the odd one out, and why?

....

....

6 These are formulae for either an area or a volume of different objects.

Letters a, b, c, … stand for lengths and π has its usual value.

State whether each formula is for an area or a volume.

a $\pi r^2 h$ ....

b $\frac{3\sqrt{3}}{2}s^2$ ....

c $2\pi r(r + h)$ ....

d $\frac{4}{3}\pi abc$ ....

e $\frac{1}{2}(a + b)h$ ....

f $\frac{1}{3}\pi r^2 h$ ....

g $\frac{\pi d^2}{4}$ ....

h $\frac{\sqrt{2}}{12}a^3$ ....

i $\frac{h}{3}(a^2 + ab + b^2)$ ....

j $2(1 + \sqrt{2})s^2$ ....

7 In these formulae p and q are lengths. M could be a constant, a length or an area.

State which it is in each case.

a area $= M(p + q)$ .... M is ....

b volume $= M(p^2 + q^2)(p - q)$ .... M is ....

c length $= \dfrac{pqr}{M^2}$ .... M is ....

d area $= \dfrac{mq^2}{pr}$ .... M is ....

8 V is an expression for a volume, A is an expression for an area and L is an expression for a length.

What would the following be expressions for?

a $3A$ ....   **b** πAL ....

c $\dfrac{V}{4A}$ ....   **d** $\dfrac{A^2}{L^2}$ ....

9 Magnus says: 'If πd is an expression for a length, then πd^2 is an expression for an area and $\pi^2 d^2$ is an expression for a volume.'

Magnus is not correct. Write a correct version.

....

....

10 A formula for the area of a triangle with sides of length a, b and c is:

$\sqrt{s(s - a)(s - b)(s - c)}$ where $s = \dfrac{a + b + c}{2}$.

a Explain why s must be a length. ....

....

b Show that the formula gives the correct answer for the area of this right-angled triangle, where all lengths are given in the same units.

....

....

....

c Explain why the formula must be a formula for an area.

....

....

....

1 a Explain why all squares are similar but not all rectangles are similar.

....

....

b Are all circles similar? Give a reason for your answer.

....

....

2 In the triangle, EB is parallel to DC.

a Work out the length of ED.

....

....

b Work out the length of BC.

....

....

3 ABCD is a rhombus.

a Show that the four small triangles are congruent.

....

....

....

....

....

....

b Use this fact to show that the diagonals AC and BD are perpendicular.

....

....

4 **a** Calculate the value of x.

....

.... $x =$ ....

b Calculate the value of y.

....

.... $y =$ ....

y cm, 63°, 4.5 cm, 27°, x cm

5 An A4 sheet of paper is 29.7 cm long and 21.0 cm wide.

a Calculate the value of a.

....

....

.... $a =$ ....

b Calculate the size of the acute angle between the diagonals of the rectangle.

....°

29.7 cm, a°, 21.0 cm

6 **a** Angles ABC and BDC are right angles.

Show that triangles ABC, ADB and BDC are all similar.

....

....

....

B, 24.0 cm, A, D, 35°, C

b Calculate the length of BD. ....

.... BD = ... cm

c Calculate the length of AB. ....

.... AB = ... cm

7 **a** Calculate the value of a.

....

.... $a =$ ....

b Calculate the value of b.

....

.... $b =$ ....

5 cm, 5 cm, 8 cm, a°, b°

8 The diameter and the height of a food can are both a cm.

Formulae for the surface area, volume and total rim length – but not necessarily in that order – are $2\pi a$, $\dfrac{\pi a^3}{4}$ and $\dfrac{3\pi a^2}{2}$.

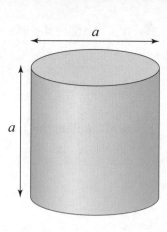

a

a

a Calculate the surface area, if $a = 10$.

....

....

.... surface area = ...

b If the volume in cm³ has the same numerical value as the area in cm², what is the value of a?

....

.... $a =$ ....

9 These are formulae for surface areas and volumes of some common solid shapes. The letters a, h, r and s are lengths. State whether each formula is for area or volume.

a $\dfrac{4}{3}\pi r^3$ ....

b $a^2 + 2as$ ....

c $4\pi r^2$ ....

d $\dfrac{ha^2}{3}$ ....

e $\pi r(r + s)$ ....

f $\dfrac{1}{3}\pi r^2 h$ ....

10 ABCD is a rectangle. P, Q, R and S are the mid-points of the sides.

How many shapes can you find that are:

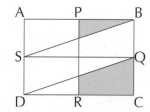

a congruent to the shaded triangle

....

b similar to the shaded triangle but not congruent to it

....

c congruent to the shaded trapezium

....

d similar to the shaded trapezium but not congruent to it.

....

11 The lighthouse is 9.6 km east of a point on the beach and 7.5 km north of it.

A boat sails directly from the same point on the beach to the lighthouse.

Calculate the distance and the bearing of the boat's journey.

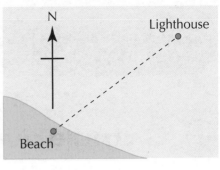

....

....

.... distance = ... km and bearing = ...°

12 **a** Show that this is a right-angled triangle.

....

....

b Calculate the size of the smallest angle.

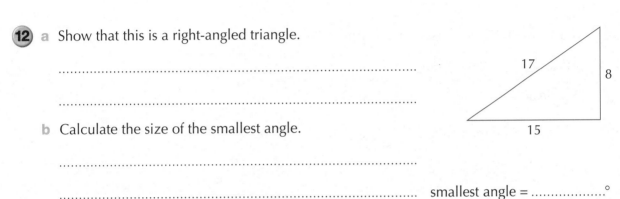

....

.... smallest angle = ...°

13 A ladder, 2.40 metres long, is leaning against a wall.

For safety, A should be about 75°.

a Find the distance of the foot of the ladder from the wall if A is 75°.

.... distance = ... m

b Find the value of A if the foot of the ladder is one metre from the wall.

.... A = ...°

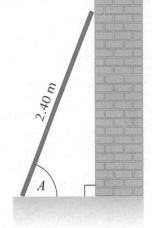

14 In these formulae a, b and c are lengths.

State whether each expression is for a length, an area or a volume.

a $\dfrac{ab + bc + ca}{a + b + c}$ .... **b** $\dfrac{a^2c^2}{4b}$ ....

c $5\pi^2 a$ .... **d** $\sqrt{2}a(b + 3c)$ ....

Handling data

14 Cumulative frequency

In this section you will estimate and find the median, quartiles and interquartile range for large data sets, including using a cumulative frequency diagram.

1 This table shows the masses of 240 young children.

Mass (kg)	10 ≤ mass < 12	12 ≤ mass < 14	14 ≤ mass < 16	16 ≤ mass < 18	18 ≤ mass < 20
Frequency	56	44	90	36	14

a Estimate the median mass.

....

....

....

b What can you say about the range?

....

....

....

2 This table shows the ages of a group of 160 people in a cinema.

Age	16–20	21–24	25–34	35–44	45–59	60 or over
Frequency	12	32	27	55	13	21

a Find, as accurately as you can:

i the age of the youngest person ....

ii the age of the oldest person ....

iii the lower quartile of the ages. ....

b Explain why the interquartile range cannot be less than 11 years.

....

....

3 This cumulative frequency graph shows the times taken by 360 people to complete a fun run.

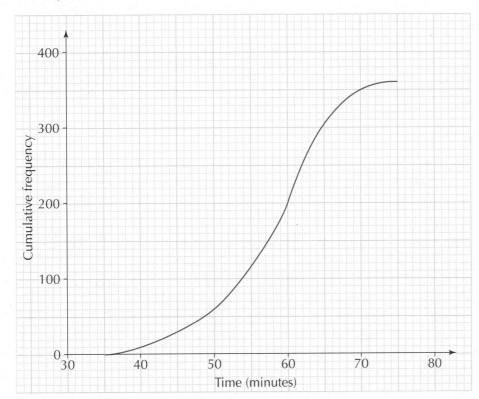

a What was the median time?

....

b How many took less than 50 minutes?

....

c How many took more than an hour?

....

d What was the interquartile range?

....

....

....

....

4 This stem-and-leaf table shows the ages of a group of adults.

Find:

2	333558
3	000112224589
4	11122567777
5	011489
6	356
7	1158

a the median age

Key   4 | 2 = 42 years old

....

b the range of ages

....

c the upper quartile

....

d the interquartile range.

....

5 This table shows the daily income for a group of workers.

Income (£)	140–	150–	160–	170–	180–	190–200
Frequency	3	10	12	20	25	10

a Draw a ~~cumulative frequency curve~~ bar chart to illustrate this data.

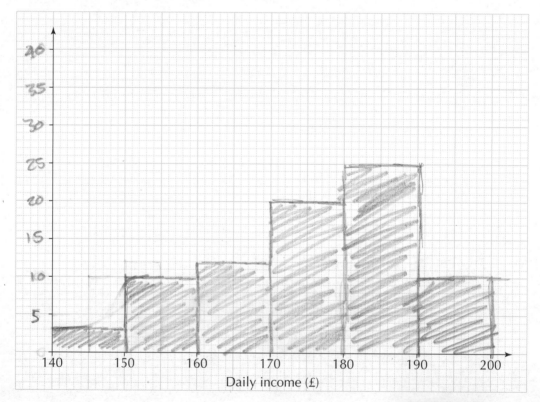

b Use your graph to estimate:

i the median income ....

ii the interquartile range. ....?.......

6 This box plot shows the results of a survey of journey times.

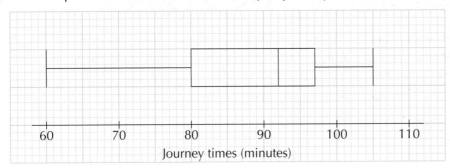

Journey times (minutes)

a Find the shortest journey time. ....

b Find the median journey time. ....

c Find the interquartile range. ....

d What percentage of people had a journey lasting more than 80 minutes? ....

7 This cumulative percentage curve shows the distribution of marks in a national exam. The maximum possible mark was 120.

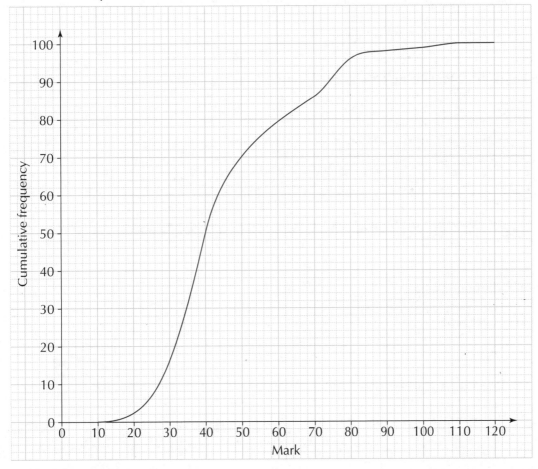

a Find the median mark. ....

b What percentage of candidates scored 80 or less? ....

c The pass mark was 30. What percentage passed? ....

d Estimate the interquartile range. ....

Comparing distributions

In this section you will compare two or more distributions and make inferences, using the shape of the distributions and measures of average and spread, including median and quartiles.

7

1 Here are the test marks for two groups of students.

Mark	0–10	11–20	21–30	31–40	41–50	51–60
Group A	25	48	67	51	48	9
Group B	32	72	150	240	101	85

a What is the modal class for Group A? ....

b Which group has the lower median? ....

c Which group did better on the test? ....

8

2 Here are the box plots for two distributions.

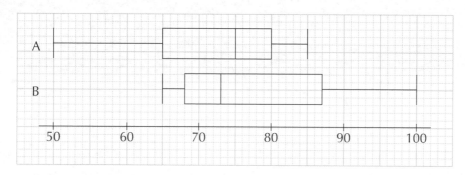

Which distribution has:

a the larger range ....

b the larger median ....

c the larger interquartile range ....

d a positive skew? ....

3 This frequency diagram shows the results of students who took an English test.

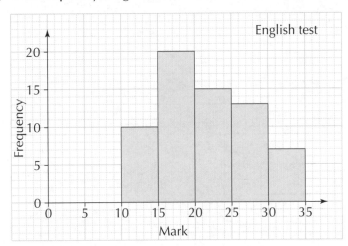

Here are the same students' results for a science test.

Mark	10–	15–	20–	25–	30–35
Frequency	5	9	16	17	13

a Draw a similar frequency diagram to show the results of the science test.

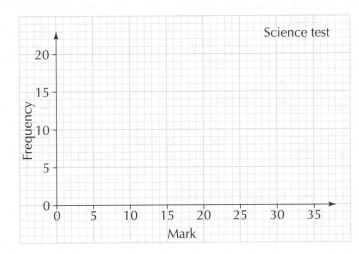

b On average, on which test did the students get better marks?

Give a reason for your answer.

....

....

....

> **Exam tip**
> Find appropriate statistics, e.g. median.

4 Match the correct box plot to each of these descriptions.

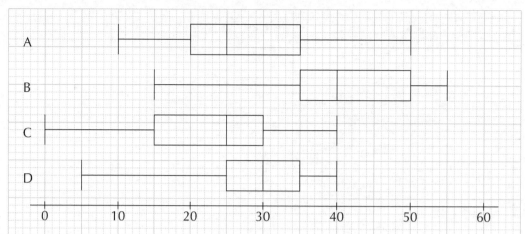

a The interquartile range is 15 and the median is 45. ....

b The range is 40 and the lower quartile is 15. ....

c The upper quartile is 35 and there is a negative skew. ....

5 Do these two diagrams represent the same distribution?

Give a reason for your answer.

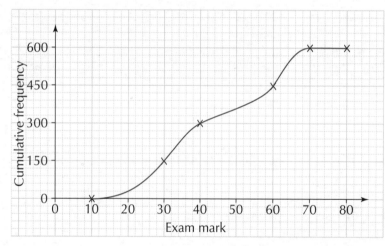

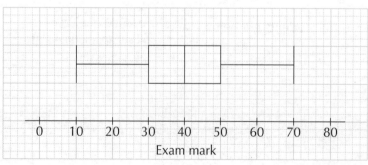

....

....

6 Here are two cumulative frequency curves.

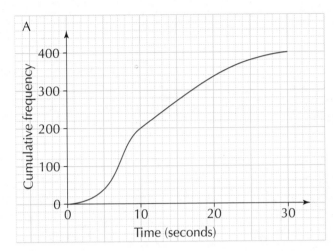

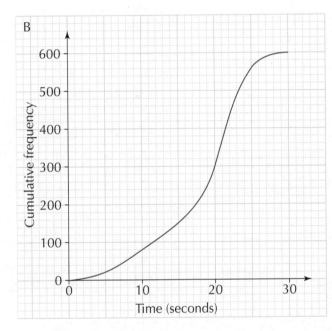

Compare these two distributions, working out any appropriate statistics.

....

....

....

....

....

....

....

7 Here are two frequency distributions.

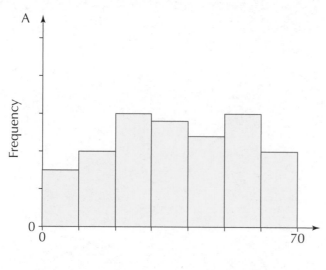

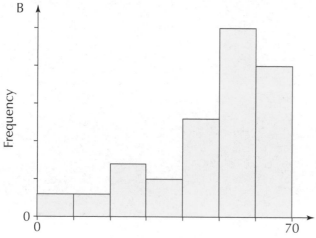

a What can you say about the medians? ....

....

....

....

b What can you say about the interquartile ranges? ....

....

....

....

Probability

In this section you will show that you know when to add or multiply two probabilities.

1 Here are the results of a survey of when a bus arrives each weekday morning over an 8-week period.

On time	Up to 5 minutes late	Over 5 minutes late
28 days	8 days	4 days

What is the probability that the bus will be:

a on time .... **b** more than 5 minutes late .... **c** late? ....

2 a A dice is thrown.

What is the probability of not getting a six? ....

b A dice is thrown twice.

What is the probability of not getting a six?

....

c Now generalise this result for three dice.

....

....

3 Twenty cards are numbered from 1 to 20. One card is taken at random.

a Find the probability that it is:

i a multiple of 3 .... **ii** multiple of 7 ....

iii a multiple of 3 or 7. ....

b A student writes:

The probability of a multiple of 4 is $\frac{1}{4}$.

The probability of a multiple of 5 is $\frac{1}{5}$.

So the probability of a multiple of 4 or 5 is $\frac{1}{4} + \frac{1}{5} = \frac{9}{20}$.

i Why is this not correct?

....

ii What is the correct answer?

....

4 An ordinary pack of playing cards has equal numbers of spades, hearts, diamonds and clubs.

   a A card is taken at random from a pack. Find the probability that it is:

     i a heart ....   **ii** not a heart. ....

   b One card is taken at random from each of two packs. Find the probability that:

     i both are hearts ....

     ii neither is a heart. ....

5 There are two sets of traffic lights on Pat's route.

The probability that the first is red is 0.3.

The probability that the second is red is 0.4.

   a Find the probability that:

     i both sets are red ....

     ii neither set is red. ....

   b What assumption have you made in calculating those probabilities? Is that a reasonable assumption in this case?

     ....

     ....

6 A spinner shows one of four colours. The colours have these probabilities.

Colour	red	yellow	blue	green
Probability	0.4	0.3	0.2	0.1

   a Find the probability that in one spin the colour is:

     i red or yellow ....   **ii** red or blue ....   **iii** not red ....

   b The spinner is spun twice. Find the probability of:

     i a red followed by a yellow ....   **ii** a blue followed by a green ....

     iii two reds ....   **iv** no reds ....

7 A dice is biased. The probability of a 1 is 0.15. The probability of a 2 is 0.2.

   a Write a question for which the answer is $0.15 + 0.2 = 0.35$.

     ....

   b Write a question for which the answer is $0.15 \times 0.2 = 0.03$.

     ....

8 The probability that a birdwatcher will see a falcon is 0.2.

The probability that she will see a buzzard is 0.6.

   a She says that the probability that she will see a falcon or a buzzard is 0.2 + 0.6 = 0.8.

      Is this correct? Give a reason for your answer.

      ....

      ....

   b She says that the probability that she will see a falcon and a buzzard is 0.2 × 0.6 = 0.12.

      Is this correct? Give a reason for your answer.

      ....

      ....

9 In a television show game, each contestant could win a top prize, one of a number of smaller prizes or nothing at all.

The probability of winning the top prize is 0.02.

The probability of not winning a prize is 0.8.

   a Find the probability of these outcomes.

      i A contestant will win a prize.

      ....

      ii A contestant will win a prize that is not the top prize.

      ....

      iii Two successive contestants will not win a prize.

      ....

      iv Two successive contestants will both win the top prize.

      ....

   b Jill says: 'If 50 people play the game then one of them is certain to win the top prize because 0.02 × 50 = 1 and if the probability is 1 it is bound to happen.'

      Is Jill correct? Give a reason for your answer.

      ....

      ....

⑰ Tree diagrams

In this section you will use tree diagrams to calculate probabilities of combinations of independent events.

7

1 a Find the probability of scoring two heads if two coins are flipped.

....

....

b Find the probability of getting two fives if two dice are thrown.

....

....

8

2 Gary throws a dice twice. He is trying to throw sixes.

a Write the probabilities on the branches of this tree diagram.

Exam tip

Always multiply along the branches and add the numbers at the end.

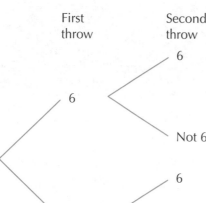

First throw   Second throw

6

6

Not 6

6

Not 6

Not 6

b Find the probabilities of the following outcomes.

i two sixes ....

ii no sixes ....

iii one six ....

iv at least one six ....

3 The probability that a train will be late on Monday is 0.1.

The probability that the train will be late on Tuesday is 0.3.

a Write the probabilities on this tree diagram.

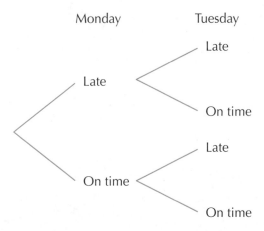

Monday   Tuesday

Late

Late

On time

Late

On time

On time

b Find the probabilities of the following outcomes.

i The train will be late on both days. ....

ii The train will be on time on both days. ....

iii The train will be late on one of the two days. ....

4 A spinner shows red with probability $\frac{1}{3}$ and blue with probability $\frac{2}{3}$.

a Complete this tree diagram to show the outcomes of two spins.

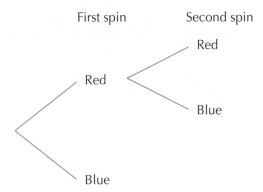

First spin   Second spin

Red

Red

Blue

Blue

b Find the probabilities of these outcomes.

i red followed by blue ....

ii one red and one blue, in either order ....

iii at least one red ....

8

5 A test has two parts, a theory and a practical. The probability that Alice passes the theory is 0.8 and the probability that she passes the practical is 0.6.

a Complete this tree diagram and write the probabilities on the branches.

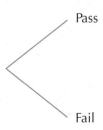

Theory   Practical

Pass

Fail

b Find the probability that Alice:

i passes both parts ....

ii passes one of the two parts ....

iii does not fail both parts. ....

6 Lucy said: 'I beat my brother at badminton 2 out of 3 times and I beat him at tennis 3 out of 4 times.'

a Lucy and her brother play a game of badminton and then a game of tennis. Complete this tree diagram and add the probabilities.

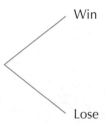

Badminton   Tennis

Win

Lose

b Find the probability that Lucy:

i wins both games ....

ii loses both games ....

iii wins one of the two games. ....

7 The weather forecaster says: 'The probability or rain tomorrow in Truro is 0.6 and in Carlisle it is 0.3.'

   a Use a tree diagram to help you find the probability that there will be rain in one of the two cities tomorrow.

probability = ...

   b What assumption did you make when you worked out the answer to part **a**?

....

....

8 The manager of a football team thinks that the probability of his team winning the next match and the one after that are 0.8 and 0.4 respectively.

Use a tree diagram to help you find the probability of their winning one of the two matches.

probability = ...

1 This box plot shows the heights of a large group of people.

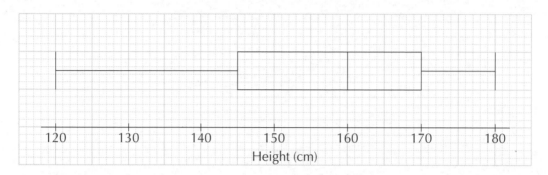

Height (cm)

  a Find the interquartile range. ....

  b One person is chosen at random. What is the probability that this person's height is less than 170 cm?

    ....

  c Two people are chosen at random. What is the probability the heights of both of them are less than 170 cm?

    ....

2 A dice has the numbers 1, 1, 2, 3, 3, 3 on its six faces.

A second dice has the numbers 1, 2, 2, 2, 2, 3 on its six faces.

Bethan throws both dice.

Work out the probability of each of the following outcomes.

Give your answers as fractions.

  a 1 on both dice .... probability = ...

  b an odd number on both dice .... probability = ...

  c not getting a 3 on either dice. .... probability = ...

3 The masses of 200 children are shown in this cumulative frequency diagram.

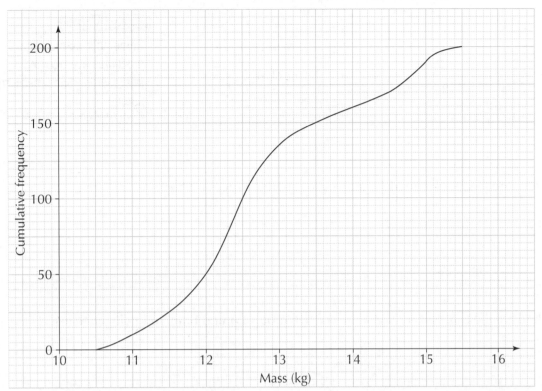

a the median mass .... kg

b the number of people with a mass less than 13 kg ....

c the number of people with a mass of more than 11.5 kg ....

d the interquartile range. ....

4 The probabilities that a long jumper will jump different distances are shown in this table.

Distance (m)	4.50–	5.00–	5.50–	6.00–6.50
Probability	0.05	0.25	0.60	0.10

a Find the probability that a jump is less than 6.00 metres. ....

b The jumper makes two jumps. Find the probability that:

i both are 6.00 metres or more

....

ii the first jump is less than 5.50 metres and the second one is 5.50 m or more.

....

5 These stem-and-leaf tables show some girls' and boys' marks for a test.

Girls

5	
6	6 7 7 8 9
7	1 2 2 5 8 9
8	2 2 5 6 6 7
9	0 1 1

Boys

5	9 9
6	0 0 1 3 4 8 8 9
7	1 2 2 5 5 6 7 9
8	0 0 0 2 4 5
9	

Key 7 | 1 = 71

Exam tip

Remember that median measures average and interquartile range measures spread.

Compare the median marks and the interquartile ranges for the girls and boys.

....

....

....

6 Here are the box plots of the scores of two groups, A and B, in an intelligence test.

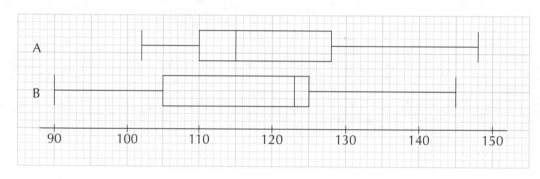

a Work out the difference between the medians. ....

b Work out the difference between the interquartile ranges. ....

....

c Does either of the distributions have a positive skew? ....

7 A test has two parts. The probability that Sonia will pass Part 1 is 0.85. The probability that she will pass Part 2 is 0.6.

Find the probability that she will pass:

a both parts ....

....

b neither part. ....

....

8 A ten-sided dice has the numbers from 0 to 9 on its faces. Adam throws the dice twice, trying to get more than 6.

   a Write the probabilities on the branches of this tree diagram.

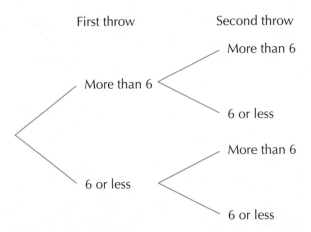

First throw

Second throw

More than 6

More than 6

6 or less

6 or less

More than 6

6 or less

   b Find the probabilities of Adam's scoring:

   i more than 6 twice ....

   ii 6 or less twice ....

   iii more than 6 just once. ....

9 The probability that Hansel will be late home is 0.65. The probability that Gretel will be late home is 0.4.

   a Complete this tree diagram and write the probabilities on the branches.

Hansel

Gretel

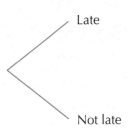

Late

Not late

   b Find the probability that:

   i both are late home ....

   ii neither is late home ....

   iii one of the two is late home but the other is not. ....

10 The cumulative frequency diagram for a set of race times is a straight line. The median is 140 seconds and the range is 60 seconds.

  a Find the upper quartile. ....

  ....

  .... UQ = ...

  b Find the interquartile range. ....

  ....

  .... IQR = ...

11 This cumulative frequency diagram shows two distributions, X and Y.

  a Which distribution has the larger median?

  ....

  ....

  b Which distribution has the larger interquartile range?

  ....

  ....

12 Sam is taking two penalty shots in basketball. The probability that he makes the first basket is $\frac{3}{5}$. The probability that he makes the second basket is $\frac{9}{10}$.

  a Draw a tree diagram to show the possible outcomes. Write the probabilities on the branches.

  b Find the probability that he will make:

  i exactly one basket ....

  ii at least one basket. ....

1 **a** Write $\frac{4}{9}$ as a recurring decimal.

....

....

b Write $0.6\dot{4}$ as a fraction in its simplest terms. ....

....

c Write $0.3\dot{2}$ as a fraction in its simplest possible terms.

....

....

2 $\frac{2}{11} = 0.\dot{1}\dot{8}$. Use this fact to write the following as recurring decimals.

a $\frac{4}{11}$ ....

b $1\frac{2}{11}$ ....

c $\frac{2}{11} + \frac{1}{2}$ ....

3 The price of a pair of shoes is reduced by 40% in a sale. The sale price is £43.50.
What was the original price?

....

.... £...................

4 House values are rising by 6% per year. This year my house is worth £180 000. Give your
answers correct to 3 significant figures.

a What will it be worth in three years' times?

....

.... £...................

b What was it worth a year ago?

....

.... £...................

5 One estimate of the total cost of World War 2 is 1600 billion dollars, where a billion is one thousand million. Write this cost in standard form.

.... $...................

6 Write these numbers in standard form.

   a $(4.8 \times 10^5)^2 = $ ....

   b $\sqrt{6.4 \times 10^{-7}} = $ ....

7 **a** $2^{-3} \times N = 2$ Find the value of N. .... $N = $ ....

   b $2 \times M = 2^{-3}$ Find the value of M. .... $M = $ ....

8 Simplify each expression as much as possible.

   a $(x + 3)^2 - (x - 3)^2$

....

....

   b $\dfrac{x^2 + 2x - 24}{x^2 - 6x + 8}$

....

....

9 A picture frame measures 30 cm by 20 cm.

30 cm

20 cm

x cm

The width of the frame is x cm.

   a Show that the sides of the picture, in centimetres, are $30 - 2x$ and $20 - 2x$.

....

....

   b Show that the area of the picture, in square centimetres, is $4(x - 10)(x - 15)$.

....

....

10 A sphere has radius r. The volume $V = \frac{4}{3}\pi r^3$ and the surface area $A = 4\pi r^2$.

a Explain why $V = \frac{4}{3}\pi r^3$ must be a volume formula and $A = 4\pi r^2$ must be an area formula.

....

....

b If the volume is 1000 cm³, work out the radius of the sphere.

.... radius = ... cm

c Show that $r = \dfrac{3V}{A}$.

....

....

11 Two formulae used in physics are $V = IR$ and $E = IV$.

a Show that $R = \dfrac{E}{I^2}$.

....

....

b Find the value of R when $E = 0.2$ and $I = 5.0 \times 10^{-3}$.

.... $R = $ ....

12 **a** Work out the equation of the line labelled A.

....

....

b Find three inequalities to describe the shaded region.

....

....

....

13 $-3 \leqslant x \leqslant 3$ and $x + y \leqslant 8$

Find the largest possible value of y.

....

....

14 A graph has the equation $y = (x - 1)(x + 1)(x - 3)$.

a Show that the graph crosses the y-axis at $(0, 3)$.

....

....

b Show that the graph crosses the x-axis at $(1, 0)$.

....

....

c The graph crosses the x-axis at two other points. Find their coordinates.

....

....

d Sketch the graph of $y = (x - 1)(x + 1)(x - 3)$.

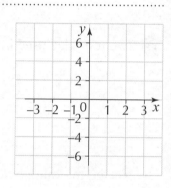

15 The volume, V, of a hemisphere with diameter d has the formula $V = \frac{1}{12}\pi d^3$.

Which of these graphs shows how V varies with d? Circle the correct letter.

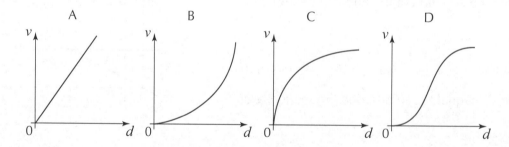

16 **a** This diagram shows two rectangles.

Calculate the lengths marked x and y.

....

....

....

.... $x = ...$ $y = ...$

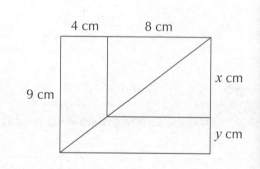

b This diagram shows two right-angled triangles.

Calculate the lengths marked p cm and q cm.

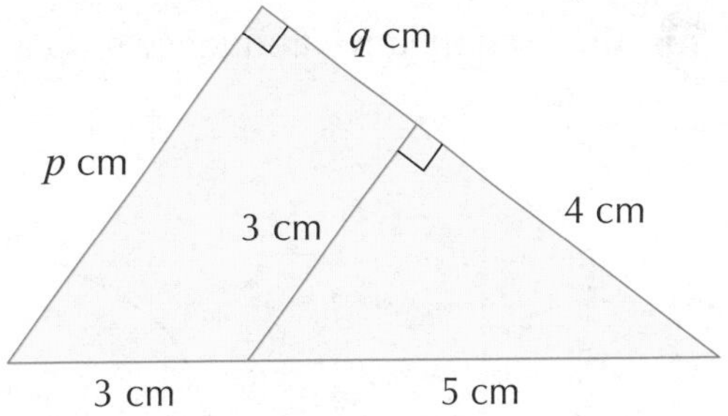

....

....

....

....

.... p = ... q = ...

q cm

p cm

3 cm

4 cm

3 cm

5 cm

17 **a** Work out the length of BC.

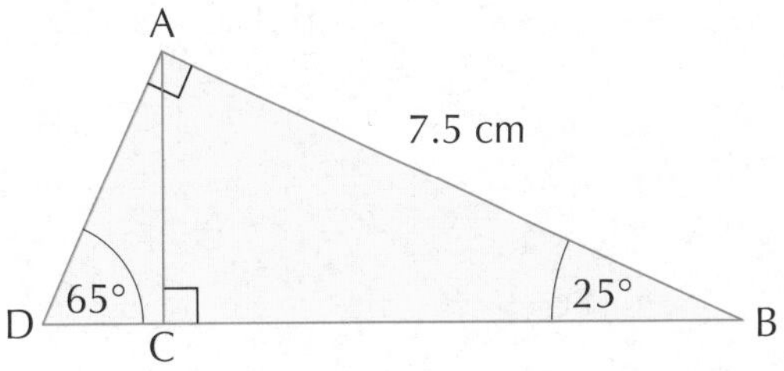

....

....

....

....

b Work out the length of AD.

....

....

....

....

c Work out the length of DB.

....

....

....

....

A

7.5 cm

65°

25°

D

C

B

18 Marie said: 'Because the two angles are equal, XY and YZ are the same length.'

Show that this is not true.

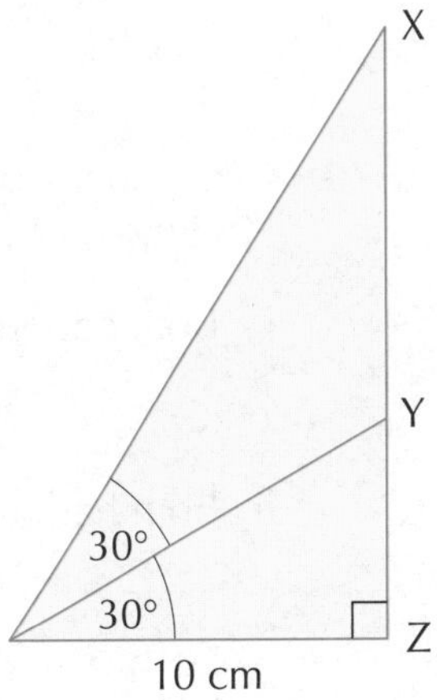

....

....

....

....

X

Y

30°

30°

Z

10 cm

19 These cumulative frequency graphs show the marks for 80 students in two different tests.

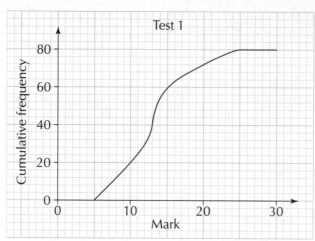

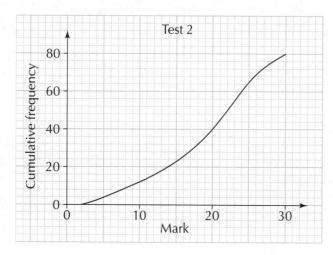

a Find the median and the interquartile range for each group and use these to compare the two distributions.

....

....

....

....

b One paper from Test 1 and one paper from Test 2 are both chosen at random. Find the probability that:

i both papers had a mark of 20 or less ....

....

ii both had a mark of more than 10. ....

....

20 Sven applies for some football tickets.

The probability that he gets a ticket for the semi-final is 0.9.

The probability that he gets a ticket for the final is 0.3.

a Complete this tree diagram by writing the probabilities on the branches.

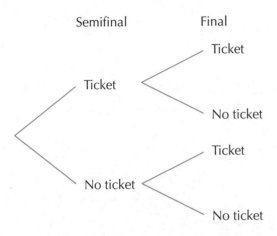

Semifinal

Final

Ticket

Ticket

No ticket

No ticket

Ticket

No ticket

b Find the probability that he gets tickets for:

i both matches ....

ii neither match ....

iii just one of the two matches. ....

21 A driving test has a theory part and a practical part.
The probability that Anna will pass the theory part is 0.9.
The probability that Anna will pass the practical part is 0.6.

a What is the probability that Anna will pass both parts?

.... probability = ...

b What is the probability that Anna will fail both parts?

.... probability = ...

c Anna takes the theory test and passes it.

What is the probability now that she will pass both parts?

.... probability = ...

22 A needle is dropped on a floor covered with floorboards.

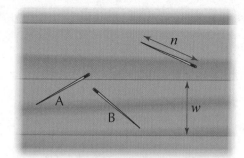

Either it will cross a line between the boards (A) or it will not (B).

If the length of the needle is n and the width of one board is w, the probability, P, that the needle will cross a line is $P = \dfrac{2n}{\pi w}$.

a Make π the subject of the formula.

.... $\pi =$ ....

b If $n = 4.5$ cm and $w = 15.0$ cm, find the probability that:

i a needle will land on a line

....

....

ii two needles will both land on a line
(Give your answer in standard form correct to 2 significant figures.)

....

....

iii neither of two needles will land on the line

....

....

iv just one of two needles will land on the line.

....

....

c A writer on the internet describes a computer simulation of dropping a needle.

He chose n and w so that $n = \dfrac{1}{3}w$.

He simulated dropping a needle 500 times and got 107 crossings.

i Explain how this gives an experimental probability of crossing a line of 0.214.

....

ii Use this to estimate a value of π.

.... estimate of $\pi =$ ....

Answers

Number

① Recurring decimals

1 **a** 4.44   **b** 535.35
   c 64.222   **d** 2.828 28

2 **a** $0.4 \times 0.625 = 0.25$

   b $2.25 \div 1.875 = 1.2$

3 **a** $6\frac{1}{4}$ **b** $\frac{1}{8}$
   c $\frac{5}{16}$ **d** $1\frac{1}{4}$

4 **a** 2.625   **b** 1.32

5 **a** $0.1\dot{6}$ **b** $0.8\dot{3}$ **c** $0.\dot{1}$
   d $0.\dot{2}$ **e** $0.\dot{5}$ **f** $0.\dot{8}$

6 **a** $0.\dot{6}$ **b** $1.\dot{3}$
   c $0.0\dot{3}$ **d** $0.1\dot{6}$

7 $\frac{3}{5}$ $\frac{1}{8}$ $\frac{3}{10}$ $\frac{11}{20}$ $\frac{49}{50}$

8 **a** 0.875   **b** $0.\dot{7}$
   c $0.6\dot{3}$ **d** $0.58\dot{3}$

9 **a** $0.\dot{4}2857\dot{1}$ **b** $0.\dot{8}5714\dot{2}$
   c $1.\dot{2}85714\dot{3}$ **d** $7.\dot{1}42857\dot{7}$

10 **a** $0.5\dot{4}$ **b** $0.0\dot{9}$
   c $1.2\dot{7}$ **d** $2.\dot{7}\dot{2}$

11 **a i** $7.5\dot{7}$ **ii** $75.\dot{7}\dot{5}$

   b $99f = 100f - f = 75.\dot{7}\dot{5} - 0.\dot{7}\dot{5} = 75$
   which is an integer.

   c $\frac{25}{33}$

12 **a** $8.\dot{8}$ **b** $4.\dot{4}$
   c 8   **d** $\frac{8}{9}$

13 **a** 36   **b** $\frac{4}{11}$

14 $\frac{2}{11}$

15

16 $\frac{4}{15}$

17 No. It does not have the same set of numbers repeating. There is an extra 1 each time.

18 0.428571, 0.571428, 0.714285, 0.875142

19 There are many possible answers. $0.\dot{3}$ and $0.1\dot{6}$ (i.e. $\frac{1}{3}$ and $\frac{1}{6}$) is one possible pair.

20 Not possible.

21 They are both correct. $0.\dot{9}$ is the same as 1.

2 Proportional change

1 **a** £13 156   **b** £345

2 60%

3 0.85

4 **a** 5.28 kg
b The multipliers are 1.2 and then 1.1, which gives an overall multiplier of 1.32, so 32% increase

5 £6749.18

6 8.64 m^2

7 17 100

8 **a i** £15 300   **ii** £11 054
b 5 years

9 **a** 500×1.3^2 **b** 500×0.8^3
c 500×0.7^2

10 **a** Increase by 4.5%
b Because the two multipliers are the same each time and the order of multiplication makes no difference.
$1.1 \times 0.95 = 0.95 \times 1.1$.

11 18.5%

12 **a** It is 20% of a smaller number of trees each year.
b 33%

13 £175.60

14 £45

15 £90

16 **a** 83.5 million   **b** 74.2 million

17 **a i** A decrease of 1%
ii A decrease of 4%
iii A decrease of 9%
b The answers are square numbers. An increase of 40% then a decrease of 40% will be a decrease of $4^2 = 16\%$, and so on.

3 Calculation problems

1 **a** 12 000   **b** 14 000   **c** 0.0027

2 0.062

3 **a** 7^{-2} **b** 7^{-1} **c** 7^9
d 7^{-6} **e** 7^5

4 **a** $\frac{8}{9}$ **b** $\frac{1}{4}$ **c** $\frac{1}{100}$

5 $c = 3, d = 2$

6 $f = 5$

7 $k = -7$

8 $n = -6$

9 **a** 10^{-9} **b** 10^{18}

10 **a** 4.2×10^5 **b** 7.5×10^{-7}
c 7.46×10^8 **d** 2.7×10^{-3}
e 9×10^4 **f** 1.2×10^{-5}

11 57.9

12 1.50×10^{11}

13 30

14 81

15 **a** Must be false   **b** Could be true

     c Could be true   **d** Must be false

16

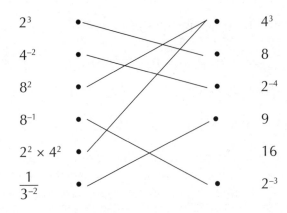

2^3

4^{-2}

8^2

8^{-1}

$2^2 \times 4^2$

$\dfrac{1}{3^{-2}}$

4^3

8

2^{-4}

9

16

2^{-3}

17 **a** $6^{\frac{1}{2}}$ **b** $6^{\frac{2}{3}}$ **c** $6^{-\frac{1}{3}}$ **d** 6^{-2}

18 **a** False, $0^2 = 0$ is the only exception

     b False, not true for the square root of any number between 0 and 1. For example, $\sqrt{0.5} = 0.707\ldots$

     c True

     d False, it is only true for positive numbers larger than 1. For example, $0.5^{-2} = 4$, which is larger than $0.5^2 = 0.25$.

19 **a** 1.70×10^{16} **b** 4.01×10^2

     c 4.07×10^6 **d** 1.60×10^{-5}

Review – mixed questions on number

1 69%

2 Using the numbers in the table, the expression works out to 2.51×10^{19} each time.

3 **a i** $0.0\dot{7}$ **ii** $0.00\dot{7}$ **b** $0.0\dot{5}$

4 **a** $\frac{10}{11}$ **b** $4\frac{6}{11}$ **c** $\frac{1}{22}$

5 **a i** $\frac{1}{9}$ **ii** 11.1% **b i** $\frac{9}{10}$ **ii** 10%

6 $m = 6$ and $n = 3$.

7 **a** $\frac{1}{5}$ **b** 2 **c** 1

8 It terminates if the only prime factors of N are 2 and/or 5. Otherwise it recurs.

9 The multiplier for three successive increases is $1.25^3 = 1.95$, which is almost 2.

10 No. Overall, there is a 2.25% decrease.

11 **a** 4.9×10^{15} km to 2 sig. fig. or 4.92×10^{15} km to 3 sig. fig.

   b About 11 million years

12 **a** 4×10^{-7} **b** 7×10^{-7}

13 Between 2×10^{-11} and 2×10^{-10} metres

14 **a** 6.7 cm **b** 16.4 cm

15 **a** The proportional increase is not the same each time. For the five ten-year intervals the percentage increases are 23%, 22%, 18%, 15% and 13% so they are gradually decreasing.

   b If you assume the increase for the next ten-year interval is 10% or 11%, the population estimate will be 7.6 or 7.7 billion

Algebra

4 Quadratic expressions

1 **a** $x^2 + 7x$ **b** $x^2 - 5x$

2 **a** $x^2 - 2x - 24$ **b** $x^2 - 2x - 15$
   c $x^2 - x - 90$ **d** $x^2 - 9x + 14$

3 **a** $x^2 + 8x + 16$ **b** $x^2 - 10x + 25$

4 **a** $(x + 2)(x + 4)$ **b** $(x - 2)(x - 4)$
   c $x(x + 11)$ **d** $(x + 5)(x - 3)$
   e $(x + 7)(x - 3)$ **f** $(x - 6)(x + 5)$
   g $(x + 20)(x - 1)$ **h** $(x - 8)(x - 2)$

5 $x + 6$

6

$x^2 + 8x + 12$ •

$x^2 - 11x - 12$ •

$x^2 + 4x - 12$ •

$x^2 + x - 12$ •

$x^2 - 13x + 12$ •

• $(x + 4)(x - 3)$

• $(x + 6)(x + 2)$

• $(x - 1)(x - 12)$

• $(x - 2)(x + 6)$

• $(x + 3)(x - 4)$

• $(x - 12)(x + 1)$

7 **a** $(x + 2)(x - 2)$ **b** $(x + 4)(x - 4)$
   c $(x + 10)(x - 10)$ **d** $(x + 25)(x - 25)$

8 It is $(9999 + 1)(9999 - 1)$

9 **a** 35
   b If A and B are two consecutive integers,
   $A^2 - B^2 = A + B$.

10 $p = 2, q = 3$

11 $r = 3, s = 12$

12 **a** $(x + y)(x - y)$
   b $(26 + 24)(26 - 24) = 50 \times 2$
   c $P = 51, Q = 49$

13 To multiply to give –6 they must be 1 and –6, 6 and –1, 2 and –3 or 3 and –2. None of these pairs add up to 3.

14 Six. They are 17, –17, 7, –7, 3 and –3

15

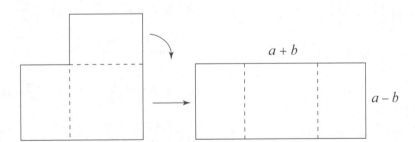

5 Algebraic manipulation

1 $x = 5$, $y = 15$

2 $x = 8$, $y = 4$

3 **a** $3x(x + 3)$ **b** $2a^2(5 - 2a)$
  c $4ab(4a - 3b)$

4 **a** $8x + 5$ **b** $5 + x$
  c $3m + 40$ **d** $2x^2 - 5x$
  e $10 - k$

5 **a** $4x^2 + 4x - 3$ **b** $15a^2 + 14a - 8$
  c $9x^2 - 49$ **d** $a^2 - 7a + 10$
  e $4m^2 + 12m + 9$

6 **a** $4x + 12$ **b** $8 - 8a$

7 Multiply out brackets or difference of two squares

8 **a** -62 and -12
  b $2x - 4 - 18 + 3x = 2x + 4$; $5x - 22$
    $= 2x + 4$; $3x = 26$; $x = 8\frac{2}{3}$

9 $x = 1.5$

10 $x = 12$

11 **a** $\dfrac{4x + 1}{10}$ **b** $\dfrac{3x - 4}{4}$

12 $c = 5$, $d = 2$, $e = 2$

13 **a** $x + 2$ **b** $x + 5$ **c** 6

14 **a** **i** $x + 3$ **ii** $2x + 6$ **iii** $\frac{1}{2}x + 1\frac{1}{2}$
  b Multiply (or divide) $x - 2$ by any number; divide (or multiply) $x + 3$ by the same number.

15 $3a(a - 5)(a - 2)$

16 **a** Simplify $4a^2 + 4a + 1 - a^2 - 4a - 4$ and factorise, or use difference of two squares.
  b $8(a + 1)(a - 1)$

17 $a = -3$ and $b = -4$ or $a = -4$ and $b = -3$

6 Deriving formulae

1 **a** $E = 1.575$ **b** $R = \dfrac{E}{I^2}$

2 **a** $P = 5a + 4$ **b** $A = \frac{1}{2}a(2a + 1)$

3 **a** $A = \pi r^2 = \pi\left(\dfrac{d}{2}\right)^2 = \dfrac{\pi d^2}{4}$ **b** $d = \sqrt{\dfrac{4A}{\pi}}$

4 **a** $s = \dfrac{v^2 - u^2}{2a}$ **b** $u = \sqrt{v^2 - 2as}$

5 $a = 1.5$

6 **a** Multiply out $\frac{1}{2}(2a + 4)(2a - 4)$
  b $a = \sqrt{\dfrac{A}{2} + 4}$

7 Find the area in two ways; either the difference between two squares or the sum of rectangles.

8 **a** $h = \dfrac{3V}{a^2}$ **b** $a = \sqrt{\dfrac{3V}{h}}$

9 Simplify $\dfrac{2\pi r}{4} + 2r$

10 **a** $h = \dfrac{2A}{a + b}$ **b** $b = \dfrac{2A}{h} - a$ **c** $a = \dfrac{9}{8}a^2$

11 **a** $f + g = 3(f - g)$
  b Rearrange the formula to get $2g = f$.

12 The area of each small circle is

$\pi\left(\dfrac{r}{2}\right)^2 = \dfrac{1}{4}\pi r^2$; subtract these from the area of the large circle.

13 $l = g\left(\dfrac{T}{2\pi}\right)^2$

14 a Because he has included a radius which is not part of the perimeter of the semicircle.

b $p = 3\pi(x+2)$

⑦ Evaluating formulae

1 166

2 66.7

3 217.5

4 11 cm

5 a The formula reduces to $V = \dfrac{h}{3}a^2$, which is identical to the previous one.

b No, it only demonstrates that it is correct in one particular case.

c 98.3 cm³

6 2.3

7 11 100 to 3 sig. fig.

8 16.4

9 14.2

10 187

11 251

12 a 137 cm³ to 3 sig. fig. or 140 cm³ to 2 sig. fig.

b $\dfrac{3}{4}\pi^3 b^3$

13 86.6 cm²

⑧ Inequalities

1 a $x \geqslant 2$

b

2 $-3 < x < 3$

3
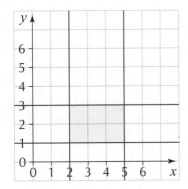

4 a P **b** Q **c** S

5 $y \leqslant 4, x \geqslant 2, y \geqslant x$

6 $y \leqslant 4 - x^2, y \geqslant 0$. Alternatively, if you are not following the convention that solid lines mean values on the lines are included, you could also use < and >.

7 a D **b** C **c** A **d** B

8 a boundary   **b** outside

c inside   **d** outside

9 a If $x \geqslant 2$ and $y \geqslant 3$ then the total $x + y \geqslant 5$ so the total cannot be $\leqslant 4$.

b There is just one point, (2, 3) in the solution set.

10 10 pairs

11 a $3 \leqslant x \leqslant 4$ and $0 \leqslant 6 \leqslant 4$

    b $x \leqslant 4$, $y \geqslant 6$ and $y \leqslant 2x$

    c $x \geqslant 1$, $4 \leqslant y \geqslant 6$, and $y \geqslant 2x$

⑨ Graphs

1 a The values of y are 4, –1, –4, –5, –4, –1, 5.

    b

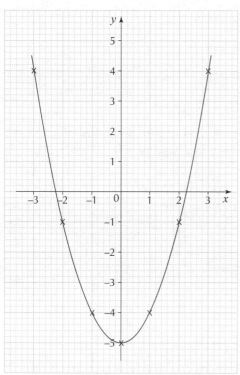

2

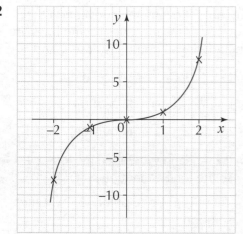

3 a The values of y are 4, 0, –2, –2, 0, 4.

    b

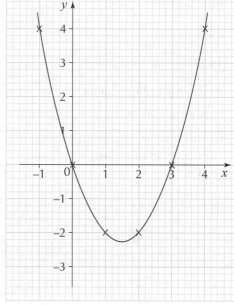

    c $x = 1.5$

4 a The values of y are 5, 3.33, 2.5, 2.

b,c

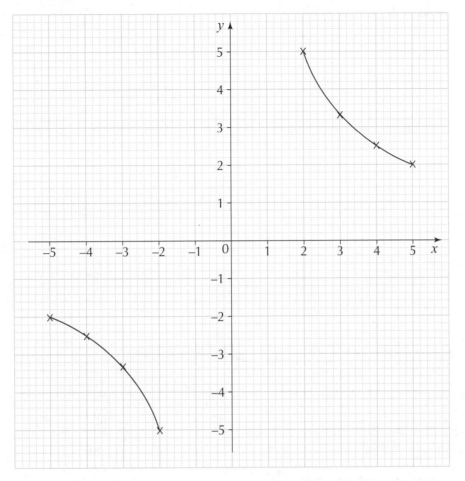

5 a C   **b** A   **c** D

6

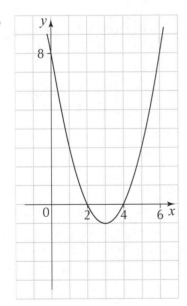

7 a The values of y are –15, 0, 3, 0, –3, 0, 15.

b

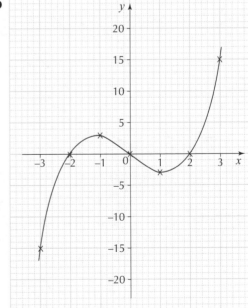

c Rotational symmetry of order 2, centre the origin

8 **a** The formula for the area is $lw = 100$.
Rearranging this gives $w = \frac{100}{l}$.

b

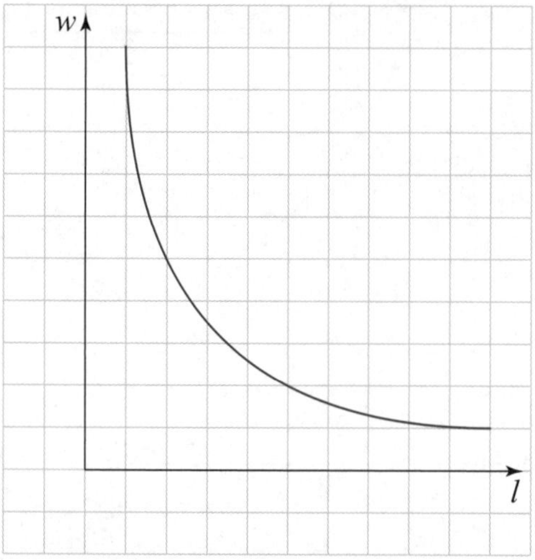

w
l

9

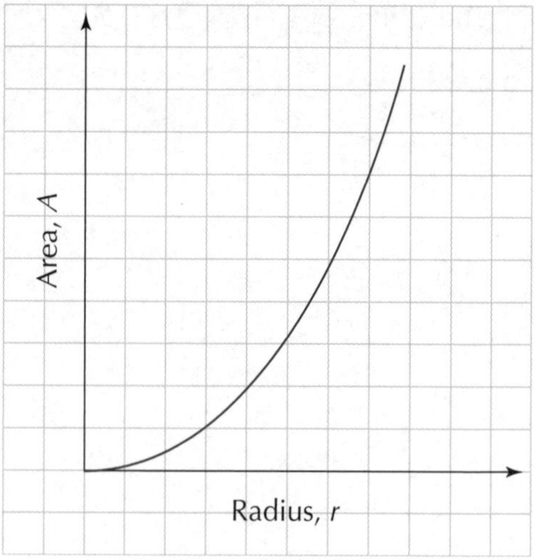

Area, A
Radius, r

10 Transforming graphs

1 **a** (0, 0) and (1, 1)

b **i** Reflection symmetry, the y-axis is the line of symmetry

ii Rotational symmetry of order 2, centre (0, 0)

2

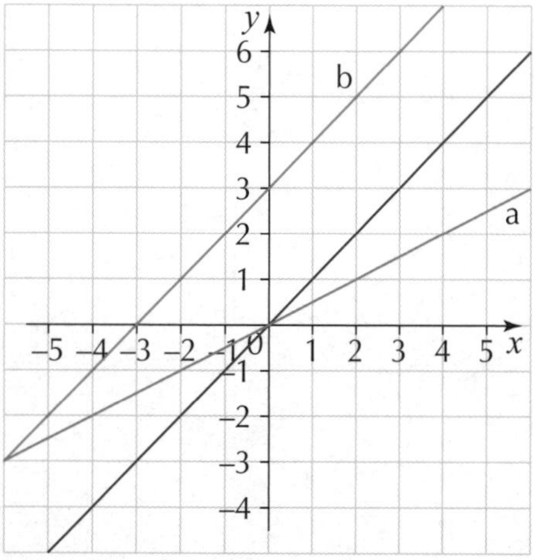

y
x
b
a

3

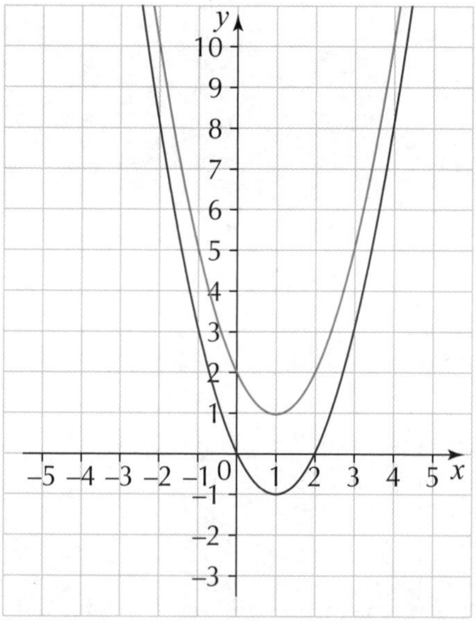

y
x

4

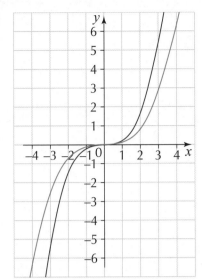

5

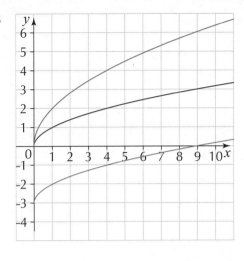

6

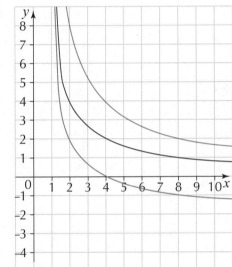

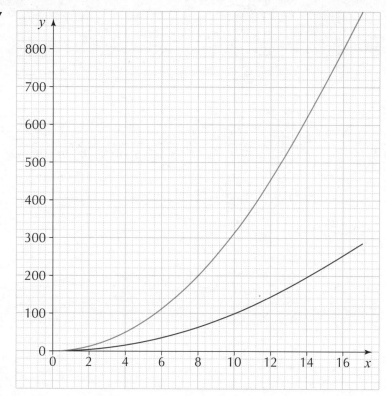

8 B is a translation of A so the shapes are exactly the same.
C is a stretch of A so the shape will be altered.

Review – mixed questions on algebra

1 **a** $(x + 9)(x - 9)$ **b** $(x + 27)(x - 3)$
   c $(x - 81)(x + 1)$

2 $4x + 3$

3 **a** $(x + 4)(x - 3)$ **b** At $(0, -12)$
   c At $(3, 0)$ and $(-4, 0)$
   d At $(0, -24)$ **e** At $(3, 0)$ and $(-4, 0)$

4 **a** 36   **b** 7

5 **a** $(x - 2)^2 - 4 = x^2 - 4x + 4 - 4 = x^2 - 4x$

   b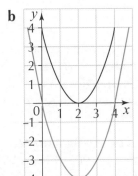

6 $\dfrac{x + 5}{x - 4}$

7 **a** $C = \sqrt{4\pi A}$

   b $C^2 = (2\pi r)^2 = 4\pi^2 r^2$ so $\dfrac{C^2}{4\pi} = \dfrac{4\pi^2 r^2}{4\pi} = \pi r^2$

8 **a** $y = x^3 - 4x + 2$

   b

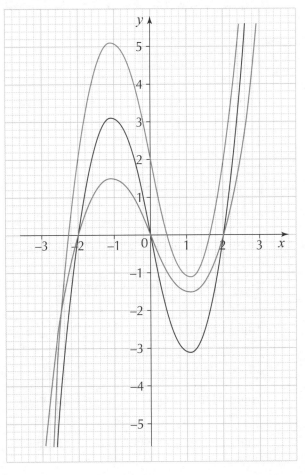

9 **a** C   **b** A   **c** D   **d** B

Shape, space and measure

⑪ Similarity

1 The shapes have the same angles and the ratio of corresponding sides is the same, 2 : 1, for all possible pairs.

2 **a** 7.0 cm

b either 6.5 cm or 7.5 cm

c either 6.5 cm or 7.5 cm

3 Angle PQR = angle PST (corresponding angles).

Angle PRQ = angle PTS (corresponding angles).

Angle QPR is common to both triangles.

This shows the triangles have angles of the same size and so they are similar.

4 Angle ADB = angle DEF (corresponding angles).

Angle BAD = angle FDE (corresponding angles).

The third angles of the triangles must also be the equal because the angle sum is 180°. This shows that triangles ABD and DEF have angles of the same size, so they are similar. Finally AD and DE are the same length, so the triangles must be congruent.

5 **a** 7.5 cm   **b** 9 cm

6 **a** 7.2 cm   **b** 1.6 cm

7 **a** All equilateral triangles have the same angles, they are all 60°, so they are similar. Isosceles triangles do not all have the same angles, so they are not similar.

b True. The angles of any right-angled isosceles triangles are 90°, 45° and 45° because two of them must be equal and the sum is 180°. This means they are similar.

8 19.2 cm²

9 The ratio of corresponding sides must be the same. In particular, using the ratio $\frac{length}{width}$,

$$\frac{AB}{5} = \frac{10}{AB}$$

Rearranging, $AB^2 = 5 \times 10 = 50$ so $AB = \sqrt{50}$ cm.

⑫ Trigonometry

1 **a** 24 cm   **b** 7.4 cm

2 **a** 28°   **b** 49°   **c** 19°   **d** 53°

3 **a** 3.8   **b** 54   **c** 20.2   **d** 82

4 **a** 9°   **b** 99 cm

5 No. The cosine of the marked angle is 8 ÷ 12 = 0.6667 and cos⁻¹ 0.6667 = 48°, not 42°.

6 One angle is 90°. If you know two other sides you can calculate the sine, cosine or tangent of a second angle and use that to find the angle. Then use the fact that the angle sum is 180° to find the third angle.

7 **a** 9.7 m   **b** 33°

8 **a** 10 cm   **b** 5.8 cm

9   8.6 km

10   114°

11   **a** In the first triangle, cos $a°$

$= \dfrac{\text{adjacent}}{\text{hypotenuse}} = \dfrac{x}{1} = x$

   b In the second triangle, cos $a°$

$= \dfrac{\text{adjacent}}{\text{hypotenuse}} = \dfrac{1}{\ } $ and if cos $a° = \dfrac{1}{y}$

this can be rearranged to give the stated result.

12   80.9 cm or 81 cm

⑬ Dimensions

1   **a** 132 cm²   **b** 60 cm³

2   **a** area, 35π or 110 cm²   **b** length, 41 cm

   c area, 12 cm²   **d** volume, 588 cm³

   e area, 83 cm²

3   **a** 12π cm   **b** 144π cm³

   c 108π cm²

4   The first is a length (a) multiplied by two numbers ($\frac{1}{2}$ and $4 + π$), which is still a length. The second is a length squared (a^2), which gives an area, multiplied by two numbers ($\frac{1}{4}$ and $4 - π$), which is still an area.

5   The fourth one, $a^2b + b^2c$, is a volume formula. The rest are area formulae.

6   **a** volume   **b** area   **c** area

   d volume   **e** area   **f** volume

   g area   **h** volume   **i** volume

   j area

7   **a** length   **b** constant   **c** length

   d area

8   **a** area   **b** volume   **c** length

   d area

9   The explanation should end: '...both $πd^2$ and $π^2d^2$ are expressions for an area.

10   **a** s is the sum of three lengths, which gives a length, divided by 2, which is still a length.

   b The formula gives $\sqrt{6 \times 3 \times 2 \times 1} = \sqrt{36} = 6$. This is the same as area $= \frac{1}{2}$ base $\times$ height $= \frac{1}{2} \times 4 \times 3 = 6$.

   c s, $s - a$, $s - b$ and $s - c$ are all lengths. Multiplying them gives (length)⁴. Taking the square root gives (length)², which is area.

Review – mixed questions on shape, space and measure

1 a Any square can be enlarged to be the same size as any other square because all the sides are the same length. Two rectangles are only similar if the sides are in the same ratio.

b Any circle, when enlarged, will give a circle of a different radius.

2 a 2 cm   **b** $2\frac{2}{3}$ cm

3 a $a = b$ (alternate angles)

$a = c$ (isosceles triangle ABC)

$b = d$ (isosceles triangle ADC)

This shows a, b, c and d are all equal.

Similarly, e, f, g and h are all equal.

This shows the triangles are similar.

Because the sides of the rhombus are equal, the triangles are congruent.

b Angles i and j are equal and add up to 180, so each angle is 90°.

4 a 8.8   **b** 9.9

5 a 54.7° (or 55°)   **b** 70.5° (or 70°)

6 a Angle DBC = 55°; angle ABD = 35°; angle BAD = 55°.

This shows that the three triangles have the same angles.

b 13.8 cm   **c** 16.8 cm

7 a 39   **b** 32

8 a 150π cm² or 471 cm²   **b** 6

9 a volume   **b** area   **c** area
  d volume   **e** area   **f** volume

10 a 3   **b** 4   **c** 3   **d** 2

11 The distance is 12.2 km and the bearing is 052°.

12 a $8^2 + 15^2 = 64 + 225 = 289 = 17^2$

b 28°.

13 a 0.62 m   **b** 65°

14 a length   **b** volume   **c** length
  d area

Handling data

14 Cumulative frequency

1 a 14.4 or 14.5 kg

 b The range is more than 6 kg but less than 10 kg.

2 a i Between 16 and 20 **ii** At least 60

 iii Between 21 and 24

 b The largest possible value of the lower quartile is 24 years. The smallest possible value of the upper quartile is 35 years. The smallest possible difference between them is 35-24 = 11 years.

3 a 60 minutes **b** 60
 c 160 **d** 11 minutes

4 a 41.5 **b** 55 years
 c 51 **d** 20 years

5 a

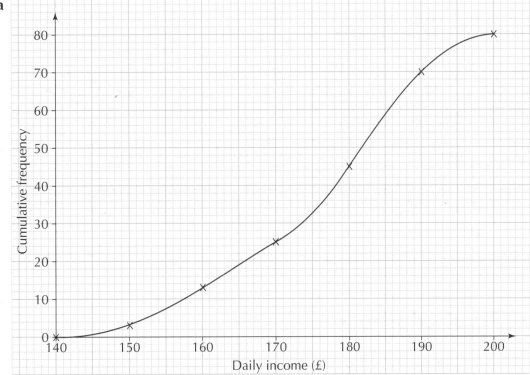

 b i about £178 **ii** about £20

6 a 60 minutes **b** 92 minutes
 c 17 minutes **d** 75%

7 a 40 **b** 96%
 c about 84% **d** about 22 marks

15 Comparing distributions

1 **a** 21–30 **b** A **c** B

2 **a** They are the same. **b** A **c** B **d** B

3 **a**

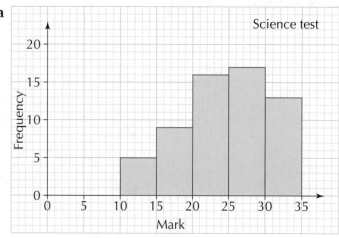

b Science. Half got more than 25 for science, less than a third did for English.

4 **a** B **b** C **c** D

5 No. They have different upper quartiles: 60 for the graph and 50 for the box plot.

6 Refer to the following statistics in the comparison.

	range	median	lower quartile	upper quartile	interquartile range
A	30	10	7	17	10
B	30	20	15	22	7

7 **a** B has a larger median than A.

  b B has a smaller interquartile range than A.

16 Probability

1 **a** 0.7 **b** 0.1 **c** 0.3

2 **a** $\frac{5}{6}$ **b** $\frac{25}{36}$

  c Probability of no sixes with 3 dice is
  $\frac{5}{6} \times \frac{5}{6} \times \frac{5}{6} = \frac{125}{216}$

3 **a i** $\frac{3}{10}$ **ii** $\frac{1}{10}$ **iii** $\frac{2}{5}$

  b i Because the results are not mutually exclusive

  ii $\frac{8}{20} = \frac{2}{5}$

4 a i $\frac{1}{4}$ **ii** $\frac{3}{4}$

   b i $\frac{1}{16}$ **ii** $\frac{9}{16}$

5 a i 0.12   **ii** 0.42

   b That the lights work independently. This will not be the case if they are synchronised.

6 a i 0.7   **ii** 0.6   **iii** 0.6

   b i 0.12   **ii** 0.02   **iii** 0.16   **iv** 0.36

7 a What is the probability of a 1 or a 2, if the dice is thrown once?

   b What is the probability of a 1 and a 2, if the dice is thrown twice?

8 a It is not correct because the events are not mutually exclusive.

   b It is correct if the events are mutually exclusive. It depends on whether the presence of one bird is affected by the presence of the other.

9 a i 0.2   **ii** 0.18

     iii 0.64   **iv** 0.0004

   b No. You cannot add probabilities in that way.

⑰ Tree diagrams

1 a $\frac{1}{4}$ **b** $\frac{1}{36}$

2 a

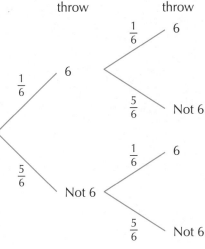

   b i $\frac{1}{36}$ **ii** $\frac{25}{36}$ **iii** $\frac{5}{18}$ **iv** $\frac{11}{36}$

3 a

	Monday	Tuesday
	0.1 Late	0.3 Late
		0.7 On time
	0.9 On time	0.3 Late
		0.7 On time

   b i 0.03   **ii** 0.63   **iii** 0.34

4 **a**

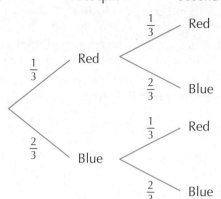

b i $\frac{2}{9}$ **ii** $\frac{4}{9}$ **iii** $\frac{5}{9}$

5 **a**

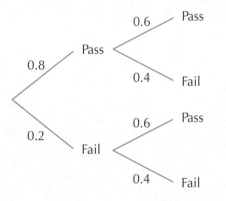

b i 0.48   **ii** 0.44   **iii** 0.92

6 **a**

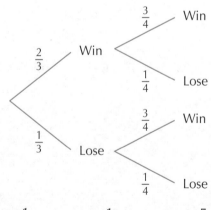

b i $\frac{1}{2}$ **ii** $\frac{1}{12}$ **iii** $\frac{5}{12}$

7 **a**

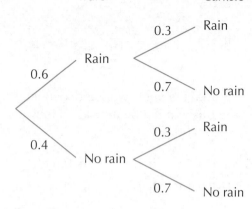

probability = 0.54.

b The events are independent.

8

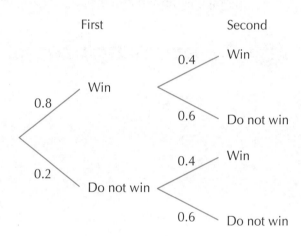

probability = 0.56

Review – mixed questions on handling data

1 a 25   **b** 0.75   **c** $\frac{9}{16}$ or 0.5625

2 a $\frac{1}{18}$ **b** $\frac{5}{18}$ **c** $\frac{5}{12}$

3 a 12.5 kg   **b** 135   **c** 175   **d** 1.5 kg

4 a 0.9   **b i** 0.01   **ii** 0.21

5 Median: girls 78.5, boys 72. The median
for the girls is 6.5 more. Interquartile
range: both 16.

6 a The median for A is 8 less than the
median for B (115 and 123).

  b The interquartile range for A is 2 less than
the interquartile range for B (18 and 20)

  c A

7 a 0.51   **b** 0.06

8 a

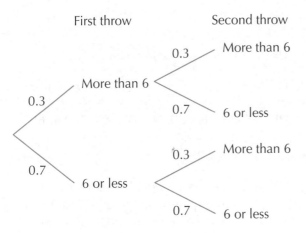

  b i 0.09   **ii** 0.49   **iii** 0.42

9 a

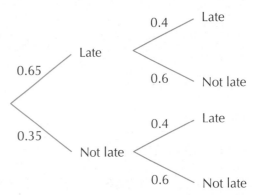

  b i 0.26   **ii** 0.21   **iii** 0.53

10 a 155 seconds   **b** 30 seconds

11 a Y   **b** Y

12 a

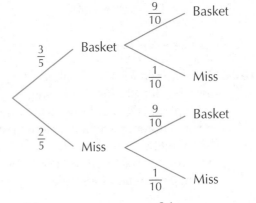

  b i $\frac{21}{50}$ or 0.42   **ii** $\frac{24}{25}$ or 0.96

Review – mixed questions on Level 8

1 **a** $0.\dot{4}$ **b** $\frac{29}{45}$ **c** $\frac{29}{90}$

2 **a** $0.\dot{3}\dot{6}$ **b** $1.\dot{1}\dot{8}$ **c** $0.6\dot{8}\dot{1}$

3 £72.50

4 **a** £214 000 (to 3 sig. figs.)
   b £170 000 (to 3 sig. figs.)

5 $\$1.6 \times 10^{12}$

6 **a** 2.304×10^{11} **b** 8×10^{-4}

7 **a** 16   **b** 0.0635 or $\frac{1}{16}$

8 **a** $12x$ **b** $\frac{+6}{-2}$

9 **a** Subtract 2 lots of x from the length and from the width to take account of the frame on each side.
   b Area $= (30 - 2x)(20 - 2x)$
      $= 600 - 60x - 40x + 4x^2$
      $= 4x^2 - 100x + 600$
      $= 4(x^2 - 25x + 150)$
      $= 4(x - 10)(x - 15)$

10 **a** The formula for V is number × length × length × length and three lengths multiplied give a volume. The formula for A is number × length × length and two lengths multiplied give an area. Multiplying by a number does not change the type of formula.
   b 6.2 cm
   c $V = \frac{4}{3}\pi r^3 \Rightarrow 3V = 4\pi r^3 \Rightarrow 3V$
      $= 4\pi r^2 \times r \Rightarrow 3V = Ar \Rightarrow \frac{3V}{A} = r$

11 **a** $E = IV \Rightarrow -= V \Rightarrow \frac{E}{I} = IR \Rightarrow \frac{E}{I^2} = R$
   b 8000

12 **a** $y = \frac{1}{2}x$
   b $y \geqslant \frac{1}{2}x$, $y \leqslant 2$ and $x \geqslant 1$.

   You could use $>$ and $<$ instead.

13 11

14 **a** If $x = 0$, $y = -1 \times 1 \times -3 = 3$
   b If $x = 1$, $y = 0 \times 2 \times -2 = 0$
   c $(-1, 0)$ and $(3, 0)$
   d

15 B

16 **a** $x = 6$, $y = 3$ **b** $p = 4.8$, $q = 2.4$

17 **a** 6.8 cm   **b** 3.5 cm   **c** 8.3 cm

18 $YZ = 10 \tan 30° = 5.8$; $XZ = 10 \tan 60° = 17.3$; $XY = XZ - XY = 11.5$ which is not the same as $Y\dot{Z}$.

19 **a** Test 1 has a median mark of 13 and an interquartile range of 5. Test 2 has a median mark of 20 and an interquartile range of 10. The marks of test 1 are lower and more clustered around the median than the marks of test 2.
   b i 0.45   **ii** 0.6375

20 a

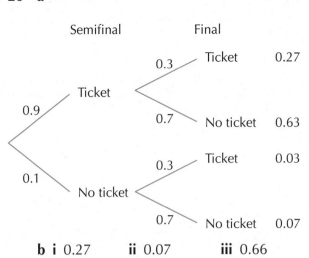

Semifinal   Final

0.9   Ticket

0.3   Ticket   0.27

0.7   No ticket   0.63

0.1   No ticket

0.3   Ticket   0.03

0.7   No ticket   0.07

b i 0.27   **ii** 0.07   **iii** 0.66

21 a 0.54   **b** 0.04   **c** 0.6

22 a $\pi = \dfrac{2n}{wP}$

   b i 0.19   **ii** 3.6×10^{-2}

   iii 0.66   **iv** 0.31

   c i The success fraction $\dfrac{107}{500} = 0.214$

   ii 3.115 to 3 d.p.